The Secret of *Forgiveness*

The Secret of Forgiveness

Justice Saint Rain

The Secret of Forgiveness
Copyright © 2021 Justice Saint Rain

Other books by this author:
The Secret of Happiness
The Secret of Emotions
Four Tools of Emotional Healing
Longing for Love
Love, Lust and the Longing for God
Why Me? A Spiritual Guide to Growing through Tests
My Bahá'í Faith
Falling into Grace
Twelve Steps and the Bahá'í Faith

Published by Special Ideas
Heltonville, IN
Special-ideas.com
1-800-326-1197

ISBN# 978-1-888547-41-2

Kiss It and Make It Feel Better 1
The Long Path to the Feel Better 4
It All Starts with the "Owie" 8
Understanding the Role of Anger 10
What We Are Angry About 19
Forgiving Our Core Sins 24
   An Exercise for Uncovering Dysfunctional Beliefs 27
Shame 35
   Projecting Our Shame onto Others 39
Forgiving Our Minor Transgressions 43
   Forgiving Our Major Transgressions 45
   Loving Ourselves 51
Forgiving Others 53
   Resistance to Forgiveness 56
Reframing Your Experiences 60
   Is It Anger, Displaced Anger, or Rage? 65
Learning Your Triggers 68
Five Steps towards Forgiveness 72
   Asking for God's Help 80
Validating the Letting Go 85
Twelve Ways to Forgive 88
Supplemental Material 90
   Training your Friends 90
   Dealing with Triggers 92
   20 Anger Management Tricks 94
   The Health Effects of Anger vs. Forgiveness 100
   Healing through Character Strengths 102
   The Secret of Depression 105
   How Can I Forgive Myself? Isn't That God's Right? 106
Prayers for Forgiveness 107
An Assortment of Quotations about Forgiveness 110

*"The practice of forgiveness
is our most important contribution
to the healing of the world."*

–Marianne Williamson

Kiss It and Make It Feel Better

When my daughter came crying to me with an "owie," I would say:
What happened?
Where does it hurt?
That looks painful.
Was it scary?
I'm sorry that happened to you.
Can I kiss it and make it feel better?
(Then I'd kiss the hurt very gently.)
Is that better?
Are you ready to go back and play?

Most of the time, the kiss would stop the crying and send her back onto the playground to play. How is this possible? Do I have magic kisses that heal wounds? Do I have band-aids up my nose and salve in my saliva?

No. I have something much better than that.

I have a listening heart.

When people are wounded, whether it is a physical wound or an emotional or spiritual wound, what they need more than anything else is a sympathetic ear.

What I did with my daughter – what most of us intuitively do with our children – is this:

Listen to the experience.
Identify the source of pain/injustice.
Validate the feeling.
Explore related emotions that might have exacerbated the perception of pain/injustice.
Let them know that their pain MATTERS to you.
Offer solace.
Confirm the pain is less.
Empower them to re-engage in life.

In short: When we are hurt, we need to know that:
The pain is real.
Our feelings are valid.
It matters to someone.

If we don't get this, then the wound does not get properly processed so that it can heal.

Sure, it may get a band-aid slapped over it, but the wound itself remains.

When a wound is not processed properly, we can't leave it alone.

We lift the band-aid off the cut.
We poke it to see if it still hurts.
We pull it apart to see if it is as deep as we remember.
We squeeze it to see if it is still bleeding.

And even days, weeks, or years later, we scratch at it and scrape the scab off – re-wounding ourselves and starting the whole process over.

Every time we remind ourselves of an emotional wound, we open it up again.

When we feed it anger, we rub salt into it.

The more angry we get, the deeper the wound gets, until it is as bad or worse than it was when it began.

Why on earth would we choose to re-inflict a wound upon ourselves?

Because we are waiting for someone to validate our feelings – to tell us that we really did get hurt, we aren't imagining things, it is someone else's fault, and we have a right to be angry.

Why do we so desperately need someone else to validate our feelings?

Because we have been taught not to trust our own feelings or to rely on our own perceptions.

Because we have been taught that we have no right to get angry, no matter what.

And because if we are wrong – if it isn't someone else's fault – then it is our fault that we got hurt. We did something wrong and deserved to be hurt.

That thought is even more painful than the original wound. *That* thought requires a different kind of processing, which we will address in a moment. For now, we will start with the premise that you are innocent.

To heal anger, to heal our wounded hearts so that we can let go of anger, we must first give ourselves permission to feel the anger. We need to hear that, yes, something bad did happen to us, and that we didn't deserve it. Yes, there is a wound under that bandage. I believe you, so you don't have to rip it back open. You can tell me about it, and I will take your side and offer you solace.

So, let me do just that:

I'm sorry that this bad thing happened to you. All of it. All 10 minutes of it. All 20 years of it.

You didn't deserve it. You deserve to be treated with respect - as a noble human being with wonderful qualities. What happened to you was wrong and unfair, and you have a right to be angry about it.

Take a moment to breathe that in and tell your inner child:
You are innocent. You deserve good things.
   They were wrong.

Breathe it in again.
You are innocent. You deserve good things.
   They were wrong.

And again.
You are innocent. You deserve good things.
   They were wrong.

When we are hurt, we need to know that:
The pain is real.
Our feelings are valid.
And that our pain matters to someone.

Your pain matters *to me.*

The Long Path to the Feel Better

To reiterate, I can see that you've been hurt.
I'm so very sorry that happened. You have a right to be angry.
Anger is a legitimate response to injustice and pain.
It wasn't your fault. You aren't imagining things or making things up.
Whatever your feelings are, they are legitimate.

Know all of this to be true.

What is also true is that every time you let yourself feel anger over the situation that hurt you, you re-open the wound and hurt yourself a little more.

When you heal the anger through forgiveness, you are able to think about the situation and take positive action without the anger or the hurt getting in the way.

So let's move on and try to heal.

Here is an outline of the ideas, or principles, that this book will address on the path from the *hurt* to the *feel better.*

(Don't worry if you don't understand or agree with everything here. I will cover it all again more slowly. This is just to give you a road map of where we are going.)

When we are wounded, we have experienced an injustice that results in a loss.

Someone has stolen a piece of our security or self-esteem through their words or actions.

Anger is a legitimate response to a perceived injustice.

Grief is a legitimate response to loss – even if that loss is purely psychological.

Feeling anger is your right.

Feeling grief is your right.

Anger gives us energy to respond appropriately to injustice.

Healthy grief allows us to let go and replace the loss of security or self-esteem from our internal reserves.

If we fail to use anger energy appropriately, and store it for future use, it turns into resentment.

If we fail to grieve, we will cling to the memory of how we lost face, instead of rebuilding ourselves.

Resentment is holding on to negative energy instead of using it for constructive action.

Unprocessed grief can cause us to hold on to negative energy for a long time.

Holding on to this negative energy is bad for our bodies, bad for our mental health, bad for our relationships, and even bad for our economic well-being.

Releasing this energy through healthy grieving and forgiveness makes it available for us to use for healthy purposes.

Holding on to resentment is your choice.

No one can MAKE you hold on to resentment if you want to let it go.

One reason to hold on to resentment is that we are waiting for our feelings of injustice and loss to be validated.

Another reason to hold on to resentment is that we are hoping to use the energy to demand restitution (a return of our lost security or esteem) or to exact revenge. It is an investment in a future resolution that may never come.

A major reason why we hold on to anger is so that we can place 100 percent of the blame for our pain on someone else. That is to say, in order for us to be innocent – for us to not have deserved the pain and loss – we feel that someone else must be to blame (even if they aren't).

Blame and responsibility are two different things. Blame is the shame or anger we attach to responsibility.

Forgiveness does not remove responsibility for hurtful behavior; it removes the shame and anger.

If you blame other people for your pain, then you are letting someone else control your emotions.

Making other people responsible for your feelings is giving them power over you.

Letting go of resentment allows you to take control of your life.

Letting go of resentment allows us to return to ourselves what we thought we had lost.

We let go of resentment, not by denying it, but by healing it.

Injustices can be global (the world is cruel), minor (he insulted me) or major (he raped me).

We can be angry at both ourselves and at other people for these types of injustices.

Everyone makes mistakes. Some mistakes are bigger than others.

You deserve to be happy and treated with respect even when you make a mistake.

Other people deserve to be happy and treated with respect, even when they make mistakes.

We heal anger by understanding and reframing it.

We heal loss by grieving and then replacing what was lost with our internal reserves.

We can reframe a hurtful situation by looking for the emotions hiding behind the anger.

We can reframe a hurtful situation by looking for the missing virtues that our emotions point to.

Reframing the situation can allow you to develop and apply needed virtues.

Reframing the situation helps you have compassion for both parties.

Reframing and compassion allow you to forgive yourself.

Reframing the situation can give you a better, healthier idea of the balance of responsibility.

Forgiving yourself makes it easier to take responsibility for your part.

Forgiving yourself makes it easier to forgive others.

Forgiving others involves healing anger and resentment.

Forgiving oneself involves healing shame.

In the chapters to come, we will be exploring each of these ideas – and several more – in greater depth. Some of them may resonate more with you than others, but each of them adds a bit of insight into the path from receiving an "owie" to going back out into the world with joy and confidence.

It All Starts with the "Owie"

Let's start at the very beginning.

Someone hurt you.

What does that mean? Most of the time, it doesn't mean that they punched you or ran over you with a car or stabbed you with a knife. Sometimes it means that they took something from you or denied you an opportunity that you felt you deserved. Most of the time, though, it means that they wounded your self-image. They were rude, selfish, insulting, demeaning, inconsiderate, took advantage of your relationship, betrayed your love (or at least your friendship), and were an all-around jerk.

In short, they did something that indicated that they considered you less than the wonderful, intelligent, noble, capable, and loving person you know yourself to be.

And you *are* a wonderful, intelligent, noble, capable and loving person.

So, what they did was unfair and unjust.

What we *need* at that moment is for someone to step in and say, "Hey, that was unfair and hurtful. You didn't deserve to be treated that way. You are a wonderful person. Even if you made a mistake, it doesn't change your innate nobility and worthiness."

What we *need* is permission to be a vulnerable human who is hurt and in need of comfort.

But that is not what we get. We get a person who acts as though they are justified in treating us badly – that it is our fault, and we deserve it. "No I didn't! Grow up! Don't be so sensitive! What did you expect? Tough luck Baby Cakes. How dare you suggest that I was mean to you!"

In other words, if we admit that we are wounded, what we receive is more attacks, so of course, *of course*, we respond instead by putting up a wall of defense.

To power that wall, we know from experience that hurt energy won't do us a bit of good, so we power it instead with anger.

Now we have called on anger energy to build our emotional wall, but anger energy fuels a physical response as well. We have all of this adrenaline running through our system telling us to DO something, and there is nothing to do. Screaming, shouting, hitting, running – these are the responses that adrenaline is designed to fuel, but they are rarely effective in adult interactions.

So instead, we do nothing, and take the hit but store the energy. In the process, we lose a little bit of good feelings about ourselves. The natural response to loss is grief, and so we grieve the loss of our self-esteem. But for most of us, we don't realize (or want to admit even to ourselves) that this is what has happened. So we keep our grief hidden behind our wall of anger. Instead of saying "they hurt my feelings, they made me doubt myself, they damaged a chunk of my self-esteem," we say, "I'm angry at them."

If we go to our friends for the comfort we need, we often find that our friends have wounds of their own and don't know how to offer compassion without it devolving into pity (which just reinforces how worthless we are) or who tell us to get over it, or who respond with their own litany of complaints.

That leaves us with unresolved grief and unused anger energy buried underneath a wound to our self-esteem. If we don't heal the wound, our anger and grief will combine to form resentment, and resentment can last for decades.

Understanding the Role of Anger

Anger is a messenger. It is a good thing. It tells us when we have experienced injustice and gives us the energy we need to fight it. Healthy anger only lasts a few minutes. It says, "Hey, this unfair thing happened. I think maybe you lost a little pride. Here is a little bit of energy you can use to build it back up again."

A healthy response to anger is "Thank you! I'll use that energy to do XYZ to make myself feel better." And then the energy is used for something productive.

An unhealthy response to anger is "Oh no! That's horrible. I'll use this energy to make them apologize so we can be friends again. Wait, they won't apologize. OK, I'll use this energy to exact revenge. Wait, I don't have the opportunity to exact revenge. I guess I'll just store this energy until I can either make them apologize or I can do something mean to them in return."

That energy then gets stored away and feeds resentment. It is like putting negative energy in an emotional bank account. It is invested in a hoped-for future outcome rather than being used to restore the loss of self-esteem today.

Healthy anger protects our self-esteem. Resentment eats away at it. To understand the difference, let's take a long look at healthy anger.

There is a school of thought that says that the secret of forgiveness is to never judge other people's actions as inappropriate so that you never get angry in the first place. But all that perspective does is shame you for having normal human emotions.

Emotions are messengers. Ignoring them or slamming the door in their face will not make them go away.

Anger is an emotional response to the absence of justice. Justice is very important, and there is very little of it in the world today. That makes anger very important. Ignoring injustice will not make it go away, nor will it give us the opportunity to correct it.

Being able to **feel** anger, **recognize** its source, **confirm** its validity, **identify** the injustice that is being perpetrated, **choose** wisely how to **respond** effectively, and then **act** in a positive way are among the most important things we can do as humans.

Let me put that in a bulleted list so you can find it later:
- Feel the anger
- Recognize its source (this is an emotional process)
- Confirm its validity (your right to have emotions)
- Identify the specific injustice (this is a rational process)
- Choose an appropriate response
- Act in a positive way

When anger is allowed to follow its natural course, it only lasts a few minutes and results in positive corrective action, even if that corrective action is nothing more than a smile and a friendly, "That's OK. I don't mind."

When your perception of an injustice is not allowed to take its natural course, it gets blocked, and the energy of anger builds instead of getting released through action. When anger lingers, it can turn into resentment or rage. That is when it stops being healthy and starts being dangerous.

Anger's natural progression can be blocked at any point along the way. Perhaps you are trying not to *feel* anger; you are having a difficult time *recognizing* its source; the *validity* of your feeling is being denied; you can't identify the specific *injustice* you are responding to; you are either having a difficult time finding an appropriate *response*, or you are emotionally attached to an inappropriate response; and/or you are unable to *act* on the response you have chosen.

Practicing forgiveness, then, is not simply about ignoring injustice or letting go of anger, it is removing the internal blocks to anger's natural progression—one step at a time—so that the anger can serve its purpose and dissipate, leaving you feeling informed, respected and empowered.

The Value of Feeling Anger

The first step in forgiving is allowing yourself to get angry.

Anger, remember, is a messenger. It tells us when we have experienced an injustice.

If we try to forgive before we listen to the message, the messenger will not go away. It will just go into hiding.

If we try to forgive before we listen to the messenger, we are ignoring the injustice. We are saying that the injustice was not real, it did not matter, or that it was not really an injustice at all.

This is really the same as saying *we deserved it*.

You see, anger is an automatic sensation, like wrinkling your nose when you smell something bad. You can't choose to not sense it; you can only choose to acknowledge it or to ignore it. If you ignore the sensation—if you pretend not to smell anything foul—then what you are telling yourself is that nothing unfair happened, that stinky is really sweet.

In order to perceive the unjust as just, and for the foul to seem fair, you must convince yourself that you deserved whatever unfair treatment you received. You are, in essence, saying, "The way I've been treated isn't so bad after all. This is normal; I deserve it. I can live with this stench for the rest of my life."

Believing that you deserved whatever bad things were said to you—or done to you—makes you feel unlovable, unworthy, dirty, or sinful. This is not healthy. We can't hold these beliefs about ourselves and still feel full of life, love, and energy. Negative self-talk, even if it is completely unconscious, drains us of hope and enthusiasm. It makes us small. It weakens us.

In other words, when we deny that we have been treated unfairly so that we can avoid acknowledging anger, we are telling ourselves that we deserve to be treated poorly. If we believe that we deserved to be treated badly in the past, then we also will believe that we deserve to be treated badly in the future.

Because of this belief, we will do things that are self-destructive, like start relationships with unhealthy or abusive people or engage in compulsive behaviors.

This is why processing anger and learning forgiveness is such an important tool for healing. It is not just about letting go of resentment. It is about releasing the depression and self-loathing that is sitting on top of the resentment, trying to keep the anger in check.

Why We Fear Acknowledging Our Anger

If anger is a natural and healthy response to injustice, why are so many people afraid to acknowledge their anger?

Here are just a few reasons:

They fear that anger will spill over into rage or violence.

They fear anger will fester into resentments that will keep them focused on the bad that has happened in their lives.

They fear that anger and resentment will cut them off from the people they love who may have unintentionally treated them unjustly.

They fear that if they show their anger, the people who hurt them will respond with anger and hurt them even more.

They have been told that "good" people don't get angry.

They fear getting angry at the people in authority in their lives—especially those who represented God—for fear it will cut them off from salvation.

They fear "rocking the boat" and attracting disapproval.

They fear damaging their family's reputation.

These are the things we fear, but that doesn't mean that they *will* happen. Even if they do, we can get past them if we focus moving *through* the anger and on to healing.

After giving ourselves permission to feel anger, the next stages are to recognize the source, to validate the anger, and to identify the specific injustice. Because recognizing the source and identifying the specifics are closely related, I will discuss both of them after explaining the importance of validating our emotional perceptions.

The Importance and Challenges of Validating Our Anger

In my book *The Secret of Emotions*, I explain that emotions are sensations that tell us about the presence or absence of virtues. For example, when we perceive generosity, we feel gratitude. When we perceive honesty, we feel trusting. And when we perceive injustice, we feel angry.

This realization is the basis for learning how to deal with anger and forgiveness. If we imagined anger to be an irrational emotion that arises for no good reason and attacks the body with uncontrollable urges and adrenaline spikes, then we would respond to it very differently.

When we see anger as a natural and healthy response to injustice, then we honor it as the messenger it is.

When we experience *any* emotional sensation, the first step is the spiritual perception of the virtue. After identifying the source of an emotion, our next step is to mentally *confirm or validate* the spiritual perception. Our mind asks, *Do I see evidence of the virtues I feel are present or absent?* With positive feelings like attraction, our mind and our heart both want to agree, even when the evidence is weak. But with anger we have the opposite response. Anger, by its nature, is a kind of accusation. When we feel anger, we are saying "someone or something here is not fair." This sets us up for resistance—both internal and external. If we are angry at a person, they are likely to say, "Hey, wait a minute! I didn't do anything wrong." If we are angry at a person we love or fear, we don't even need *them* to argue with us, we argue with ourselves. Part of us wants to defend or justify their actions so that our anger does not hurt or anger *them*, while another part of us needs to acknowledge our hurt and anger. Even if all we are angry at is a situation, there may be a little voice inside our head that says, *It is not the world's fault. If something bad has happened to you, you must have deserved it!*

This sets up a tug-of-war between our emotional perceptions and our mental need to validate what we feel. Our anger is like a rope. We try to pull the world, the other person, or even ourselves towards one perception of reality, while they try to pull us back towards another.

Until these dueling realities are resolved, until we can mentally validate our perceptions, it is impossible for us to formulate a reasonable and rational response to the situation. And until we do, we are stuck holding on to the rope, trying to pull the world into our perception of reality.

How long can we stay in this emotional limbo—angry, but not quite sure if we have a right to be?

An entire lifetime.

Just listen to people.

Anyone who feels the need to explain why they are angry is in the process of trying to convince themselves that they have a right to be. Once our head and our heart are in agreement, there is no longer any need to talk about it. It is time to move on to action.

So how do we escape this tug of war?

If we keep pulling, our anger will keep us emotionally bound to this situation forever.

If we stop pulling but don't let go, we get dragged into their perception. We are pretending that the situation was not really unjust at all, that we had no valid reason to be angry.

We are denying our reality and saying that we deserve to be treated badly. This will just lead to depression.

What is the alternative?

We can stop trying to convince the other person (or our inner voice) that we are right. We can *let them have their perception of reality*, while we look for a *different* kind of validation that our feelings are legitimate. In other words, we can let go of the rope.

When our conflict is with another person, this can be as simple as saying to ourselves, *I do not need them to agree with me on this. I can allow myself to feel slighted by this situation even if they don't think I have a reason to and will never understand my perspective.* Because we ultimately have absolutely no control over other people's thoughts or feelings, letting go of the need to convince them that our feelings are valid is the only rational path to serenity. It allows us to validate our own feelings and prepare to respond.

But when our conflict is bigger than one person or is left over from childhood trauma, then self-validation may not be enough. When we are having a tug-of-war with God, the Universe, or our own inner demons, then telling ourselves that we are right won't end the argument. These internal conflicts often involve deep, painful injustices that have never moved from anger to response because the anger was never acknowledged as legitimate. Our fingers are gripping the rope so tightly that we are afraid to let go.

In these cases, we need someone to hold on to the rope for us while we let go—someone standing on our side in the tug-of-war to let us know that if we let go, we won't be alone in our perceptions. We need someone to stand witness to the injustices we have experienced.

What does that look like?

Well, it looks like what we started out talking about at the very beginning—open, honest sharing on your part and compassionate listening on the part of a trusted friend or therapist.

Tell them that you don't want advice, just confirmation that what you are perceiving is valid. (*More on this in the supplemental material in the back of this book.*)

When someone says, "That sounds awful. That sounds really unfair. It must have really hurt. You have a *right* to be angry." What they are really saying is, "Here, let me hold on to your anger rope for a little while so you can rest and get some distance from it."

Note: you need to hear that your anger is valid *even if it isn't the entire truth*. You can't see a situation clearly until the fog of anger clears, and the fog of anger will not clear as long as it is being argued with, dismissed, or minimized. While this might seem dishonest, what you are really doing at this stage is validating your *right* to have your emotional response. (We will address the validity of our *reason* for feeling angry later.)

Once you are reassured that your feelings can be trusted, you can look at them more objectively.

With your friend or therapist holding the rope, you are free to let go of your feelings for just a moment. You can stand back and look at them more objectively. At this point, you might tell your friend, "I can see the situation differently now. I understand and forgive what happened. You can let go of the anger rope now."

On the other hand, you might say, "I'm still not ready to let go. You can hand the rope back to me. There is more processing I need to do."

Two observations:

1) Arguing over the *reason* for our anger before establishing our *right* to feel angry is why small fights can escalate so easily. When both people are wrong, neither is able to see their part in the problem until the other person's wrongs are acknowledged first. It is not so much about making the other person wrong as it is about legitimizing our own experience of reality.

2) The reason why this is so important for many people is that the most terrifying thing in the world is to fear that you can't trust your own perception of reality. The fear that you might be angry for no reason makes you work even harder to prove that you do have a reason. Once someone else validates that you do have a right to be upset, then the fear dissipates and you can consider your reason more dispassionately. Then your desire for connection, understanding, compassion and forgiveness can take over.

Once fear and anger are not clouding our judgment, we can find a rational and appropriate response to whatever situation it was that we felt was unjust.

Often, once fear and anger, guilt and depression are not clouding our judgment, we immediately realize that the most rational and appropriate response... is to forgive.

What We Are Angry About

Much of the world walks around every day in a low-grade state of anger or depression. Since many schools of thought consider depression a form of anger that is turned inward, both of these states really amount to the same thing. So why are we all so angry?

Put briefly, we are angry because the entire world has conspired to convince us that we are sinful, worthless, unworthy creatures who deserve to be treated poorly.

We live in a culture whose underlying beliefs—religious, scientific, and psychological—are that humans are fundamentally sinful, violent, competitive, and in need of fixing. In other words, the very foundations of our culture are abusive.

Think I'm exaggerating? In the dominant religion of the USA, we are told that we are born with the stain of original sin, and we need to be redeemed in order to escape death and/or damnation. In other words, life is not a gift; it is a debt. I believe that original sin is a misunderstanding of Christ's teachings, but it is the dominant perspective in the US. I believe we are "saved" from ignorance, not from punishment by God.

Even people who don't believe we are born sinful are still surrounded by people who do, as well as by cultural messages that reinforce it. In economics, we are told that people are innately selfish. In biology we are told that we are in a Darwinian battle for survival. In history we are told that civilizations are built upon war and exploitation. In cosmology, we are told that we are insignificant dots in an uncaring universe, and in psychology there is a thousand-page manual of all the ways we can be sick and almost no information about how to be healthy and happy.

In social movements, we carry the guilt of our carbon footprint and the shame of using plastic or oil or eating meat. As one friend on Facebook described us, "What else are we but a parasite, a cancer on an otherwise healthy host?"

On top of this, we have racism, classism, nationalism, and a host of other "isms" that tell us that we aren't as good as someone else.

Even if we have perfect, loving parents, unless we are trained from a very young age on how to base our positive self-esteem on the development of our virtues, these larger forces will conspire to make us question our self-worth every waking hour of the day — and even into our dreams.

In addition to humanity as a whole being seen as a blight on the planet, we are individually reminded every day that whatever goodness there might be in the rest of humanity, we clearly don't fit that mold. Maybe you are too tall, too short, too fat, too thin, have hairy legs, are bad at math, have two moms, have no mom, stutter, have super-smart siblings, have mentally ill siblings, or are obsessed with dolphins. No matter who you are, there is something that sets you apart, and our world tells us that "different" or "imperfect" is "wrong." It is amazing that any of us feel good about being human at all.

In reality, humans are glorious, noble reflections of God in need of education and guidance. But you wouldn't know that if you listen to the messages our culture bombards us with every day. That disconnection between our reality and the way the world sees us is so unjust and unfair that it is enough to make anyone who feels it very, very angry, or very, very sad.

So here is the essence of our problem:

Part of us knows that living in a culture that degrades us is manifestly unfair. That part is angry at the world and lots of individuals within it.

But there is another part of us that believes that the world is right – that we really are worthless and deserving of the worst the world has to offer. That part is ashamed, feels guilty, and is angry at *us*.

It doesn't matter whether you are mostly angry at the rest of the world, or mostly angry at yourself and being driven by shame and guilt. As long as any part of you continues to believe that you are sinful, unworthy, and deserving of shame or punishment, it will be very difficult to forgive anyone who has ever done anything to reinforce that belief.

In other words, it is easy to become angry because someone has insulted you when your anger is being fed by your subconscious belief that they are right. Once you truly believe yourself to be a good, noble, and worthy human being, another person's actions will be unable to hurt you.

For that reason, we will start our exploration of forgiveness with a focus on forgiving ourselves. Our path to forgiveness starts by uncovering and healing the destructive core beliefs and experiences that operate below the surface of our awareness. These are the ones that cause us to overreact to the day-to-day slights and injustices we experience. These are "Trigger Beliefs." We will look at how to deal with being triggered later, but first we need to discover what some of our triggering beliefs are.

Deep-seated injustices are often very old, and the range of appropriate healthy responses may be very narrow. Resentment is emotional energy that is being stored as an investment in a future outcome. It is important, then, that we choose an outcome that is within our control. Deep-seated injustices changed our beliefs about ourselves. Years later it is probably too late to change the situation that created those unhealthy beliefs. Consequently, a healthy response will want to be focused more on transforming those beliefs than on changing a situation.

Grieving the losses that these deep-seated injustices represent can be both life-transforming and painful. How does one grieve the loss of the awareness of our innate nobility? How does one grieve the loss of one's faith in oneself? How does one grieve the loss of the myth of a happy childhood? Oceans of tears may be required.

Exploring why we are angry with ourselves and uncovering the things we think we might need to be forgiven for will give us a pretty good idea of what our core sources of anger are. When we move on to forgiving others, we will have a better idea of what it is they might need forgiveness for.

Once we appreciate our core sources of anger, it will be easier to separate them from our day-to-day sources of irritation. That way we don't end up constantly being triggered — fighting life-long battles every time something upsets us. It will also be easier to choose an appropriate response.

Replacing Beliefs

One of the great truisms in personal growth is that you can't *get rid* of old habits and patterns, you have to *replace* them instead. The same principle applies to old beliefs.

These beliefs, no matter how absurd, childish, or painful, are not your enemies. They developed over time for a reason. They helped you make sense of your world and your place within it.

Once you recognize them, you need to honor them, thank them, and only then gently explain to them why they no longer apply to your life today. You want to take that old belief by the hand and walk it towards a more mature and functional perspective, not shame it out of existence.

For example, I felt responsible for my parent's divorce. It would be easy to tell myself, "Don't be stupid. It isn't your fault, so just get over it." But then my sense of responsibility would just go into hiding.

Instead, I can tell myself that every child of a divorce feels responsible—that children see themselves as the center of the universe and interpret parental behavior accordingly. I can remind myself that children need to feel that the universe makes sense and that things don't happen without a cause. It was safer to believe that I was the cause than to believe in a chaotic world.

I can find all of the reasons why I was sure that I was to blame, and then—only then—go back and assure myself that I can know better now. As an adult I can understand adult motivations, I can see the bigger picture, I can put my childhood fears in perspective. I can encourage myself with the thought, *Thank you for helping me make sense of the world, but look at how much more sense the world can make if we look at it this way.*

If you are having a difficult time finding replacement beliefs for these old sources of guilt, a professional therapist can help you find an alternative perspective with which to comfort and educate your inner child.

Recognizing and then letting go of the guilt will likely be accompanied by copious amounts of tears. Many of us have been holding in a lot of guilt for a long time. We were afraid that if we ever actually admitted what we felt guilty for, we would be proven guilty and punished accordingly. After all, what is the punishment for not being worthy to live? Why would we ever want to risk finding out?

The process of forgiving ourselves follows the pattern of feeling our anger and guilt, *recognizing* the source, *validating* our inner child's right to feel these feelings, but then *identifying* the specific injustices that we blamed ourselves for and *changing our beliefs* about them so that we no longer feel the need to punish ourselves. The choice we made was to validate the emotion but redefine the injustice. Our *action* is to educate ourselves and let go of our need for punishment.

Forgiving Our Core Sins

Just as we have suffered global, minor, and major injustices, we believe ourselves to be guilty of global, minor, and major sins for which we need to be forgiven. Addressing the biggest sins we believe ourselves guilty of first will make dealing with the smaller sins easier.

Feeling angry with ourselves, feeling guilt, and feeling shame are not exactly the same, but they are very close siblings. When we make a mistake, we feel shame. If we know it is a mistake before we do it, then we feel guilt. In practice, you might not be able to tell them apart. Healing one will help heal the others.

John Bradshaw, the author of *Healing the Shame That Binds You*, says that the difference between healthy shame and toxic shame is that with healthy shame, you know you've *made* a mistake. With toxic shame, you believe that you *are* the mistake.

We could say something similar about *feeling* guilty and *being* guilty. We feel guilty when we commit a sin—that is, we do something that we know in advance is hurtful to ourselves or others. We are guilty when we feel that we are the sin—that our very existence is a stain on the world, and there is nothing we can do to change that.

Toxic Shame tells us that we are a mistake and must change who we are to be acceptable. Toxic Guilt tells us that we are sinful—that we have committed an unforgivable injustice—and we must be punished before we will be acceptable.

The way we punish ourselves is to refuse to forgive ourselves. We commit to remaining angry with ourselves—even when we have no idea of what it is we have done wrong or why it is we are wrong.

Remember, our entire culture *tells* us that there is something wrong with us. We didn't make this feeling up. Our culture may have a veneer of rainbows and unicorns and kitty cat memes, but those are just there to paper over the core message that we are evil, selfish, smell bad, are too fat, too short, too dark, too stupid, too foreign, too poor, too ugly, too insignificant to be worth anything.

As children, most of us absorbed this sense of "wrongness" and tried to make sense of it. We created elaborate explanations as to what our sins might be. Just because we can't remember what those explanations were doesn't mean that we don't still believe them. Until we forgive them, we will continue to live in anticipation of an unspecified punishment every single day.

The big question is: what do we believe we are guilty of? What kinds of things must we be telling ourselves in order to justify carrying around this burden of unforgiven guilt?

For those of us who live with guilt and anger, we have a conscious awareness of many little sins that we are guilty of, but these often just serve to hide a bigger sin from our awareness. For example, we use all of the people we've hurt in relationships as an explanation of why we are so evil, rather than asking ourselves why we are afraid to commit to a relationship in the first place. If we can find a way to name these big sins, then we shine a light on them. When we do that, we usually discover that they are either something that we have made up, they are misunderstandings, or they are exaggerated. Naming the "sins" that we have been hiding from ourselves for years often exposes them as laughable.

As children, we believe ourselves to be the center of the universe, so in our attempts to make sense of the confusing events of our lives, we take responsibility for everything that goes wrong.

> *"Children are nonlogical. This is manifested in what has been described as 'emotional reasoning.' I feel a certain way, therefore it must be this way. If I feel guilty, I must be a rotten person. Children think egocentrically, which is mani-*

fested in their personalizing everything. Egocentricity is a natural condition of childhood, not a sign of moral selfishness. Children are just not fully capable of taking another person's point of view." – John Bradshaw

I don't know what you feel guilt for, but I felt guilty for: being born (original sin and all of that stuff), being born a male, wetting the bed, causing my parent's divorce, letting my sister be sent away to a children's home when I was obviously the one who was defective, allowing women to fall in love with me knowing I would break their hearts because I was defective and unable to meet their needs, and for taking up space on the planet when there were so many more worthy souls who deserved my place.

On top of these major sins, I added a daily list of every failure to anticipate the needs and expectations of the women around me—because they were proof positive of my biggest sin of all: I didn't love and care for other people enough to earn my place in the world. Life was not a gift, it was a debt, and I was failing to make my daily payments. I was guilty, and I couldn't forgive myself.

All of these "sins" seem funny to me now that I have given them a name. They are absurd. No sane person would believe them. Yet I can assure you that these, and many more just like them, rattle around in the heads of most people. If they *didn't*, then most people would behave much differently than they do. Consider, for example, the popularity of such songs as "Highway to Hell" and "Bad to the Bone" or video games such as *Grand Theft Auto*. These were created *by* and *for* people who have given up on believing that they are forgivable.

If people liked themselves, if people forgave themselves for their imperfections, then people would treat themselves and each other with more kindness and respect. Not only that, but the whole question of forgiving others would be simple. We would see them as the same noble, worthy, and forgivable people that we are.

An Exercise for Uncovering Dysfunctional Beliefs

In order to forgive and let go of an inaccurate belief about yourself, you need to know what it is. There is an exercise I recommend— "Internal Consultation"—in which you try to get in touch with inner emotions and sensations. This same technique can help you get in touch with the beliefs behind your feelings of guilt and anger and create an opportunity for forgiveness.

Internal Consultation is a powerful tool for identifying the message of the sensations that your emotions are generating. It does not require money, tools, or even a therapist, although a therapist can often be helpful. If it sounds similar to other techniques you've used, it probably is. It isn't rocket science, but it can certainly take you places.

Here are the basics:

Sit quietly and comfortably.

Close your eyes if you like.

Become aware of your body.

Check for any sensations.

Be open to sensations that you can't put your finger on or give a name. Pay particular attention to the area around your throat, heart, chest, and stomach. Check for sensations that might signal stress, like tightness, heaviness, heat, and pain. Also check for sensations that might signal positive reactions like lightness, warmth, and calm.

When you become aware of a physical or emotional sensation, don't pounce on it. Approach it as you would a butterfly. Your goal is to give it a name or hear its message, not to grab it and shake it.

The meaning of the sensation may not come to you in words, so be open to other forms of communication.

Become aware of your inner vision – your visual imagination.

Check for any images or pictures that might come to you.

Be open to images glimpsed out of the corner of your mind's eye.

Be aware of your inner voices – there may be many, like a little community.

Check for any voices that would like to be heard.

Be open to random phrases, lines from songs or poems, quiet voices.

If anything comes to you, welcome it. If it has a name, say hello. If you're not sure of its name, ask open-ended questions to find out what it is and what it wants to communicate with you.

This is not an interrogation.

It is similar to what is often referred to as inner-child work, but what you hear won't necessarily be a child. You will want to maintain an attitude of welcome acceptance, curiosity, tenderness, empathy. Often, once you have a sense of what is present, all you will need to do is sit with it comfortably. Its presence is its own message – no more need be said. At other times, you will want to explore what is behind or accompanying a presence.

This process is called internal consultation rather than internal listening because you are trying to create a relationship with this part of you that has something to share. Whatever it has to share is always true – for that part of you – but not necessarily true for all of you. It is important to give it a voice without giving it power over you.

This feeling, sensation, belief, experience, or observation deserves to be heard, but you are under no obligation to agree with it. In fact, the whole point of using this process is to uncover feelings and beliefs that have been misunderstood or have led you in unhelpful directions. The goal is not to accept them or reject them, but rather to gently guide them towards understandings that are more mature and consistent with your current vision. This is a process of guidance and education, not coercion.

Often is it enough to just acknowledge a feeling or thought without trying to change it or give it advice. This is because many times the message that a feeling is trying to send is simply, "I'm here!" Simply saying hello to it can release the energy that has been trying to get your attention.

If you've had any experience with working with a good therapist, then you may identify with this scenario. You can be in turmoil all week because of some event or personal interaction. You are sure it is going to take hours to work through with your therapist, but after hearing just a few minutes of your ranting, your therapist says, "It sounds to me like you might be feeling ___." And instantly the turmoil is gone. You've been heard. That's all you needed.

When we learn how to do this for ourselves, we can save ourselves a lot of turmoil (and therapy sessions).

I'm reminded of the scene in the movie "It's a Wonderful Life" in which George Bailey's young son follows him around, pulling on his coattails, saying, "Excuse me" at successively higher volume until George finally turns in exasperation and says, "Excuse you for what?" To which the child replies, "I burped."

Like a burp that is not nearly as annoying as the bellowed request to be excused, the fears, transgressions, and concerns that generate powerful internal sensations are often of much less significance than the irritation they generate when they are not acknowledged.

Even when the issues are of great importance, the resolution may not require any intervention because the "you" who is uncovering the issue has more internal resources than the "you" who generated the issue. In other words, issues that were buried when you were a child because you didn't have the emotional resources, cognitive ability, and life experience to deal with them are now easy to handle – once they have a name.

Another reason why simply acknowledging a feeling can instantly resolve tension has to do with the nature of emotions themselves. Emotions tell us about the presence or absence of virtues in our lives. Simply naming the emotion can help us understand our situation more clearly and resolve all sorts of inner turmoil.

For example, sadness tells us that we perceive the loss of a source of goodness in our lives. It tells us, "You did have access to this source of virtue; now you don't." In order to hide sadness from ourselves, we must convince ourselves that either A) the thing we have lost isn't really gone, or B) the thing we lost didn't really have any value to us in the first place.

Any time we try to convince ourselves that something we love isn't really valuable, the part of us that loves goodness is going to start screaming at us. It will jump up and down, it will grab hold of our heart, our throat, or our stomach, and start squeezing.

If we want this tightness to go away, all we have to do is say, "I'm sad about ___." In doing so, we are admitting that we have lost something of value. Once we acknowledge that something has value to us, it is often much easier to accept the fact that it is gone and get on about the business of finding some other source of goodness to fill the void. So acknowledging sadness can make it go away. It's not magic. It's just dismissing the messenger after the message has been delivered!

If naming an emotion doesn't instantly clarify the nature of the message behind it, you might want to ask any strong emotional sensation what virtue or attribute it is responding to. There are, of course, some sensations that will require more than a name. They may be associated with traumatic experiences, major life events, long-term perspectives, or family systems. It is OK to call a feeling "something" and just sit with it to see what it has to share.

When you are done, say thank you and ask if it is all right to move on.

Then write down whatever of value you can put into words while the new awareness is still fresh. This could be a memory, feeling, experience, virtue, or new awareness. You don't have to be completely coherent or clear, just get it onto paper. Creating an objective record of your internal experiences will help make them real and give you something to refer back to if your new-found understandings start to get cloudy.

When we write down the things we think, feel and remember, it gets them out of our heads. As long as they are in the echo chamber of our minds, they seem loud and big and important. Once they are down on paper, they no longer seem so huge or powerful. In fact, your sins, fears, and worries may look just as silly as mine did.

Some additional tips and tricks:

The goals of Internal Consultation are to receive the message and to honor the messenger, not to become overwhelmed by either of them. The advantage of naming a sensation or an awareness is that it establishes a distinction between you and it. It creates a safe distance between you.

Don't eat or drink while practicing Internal Consultation. Physical sensations often serve double-duty. Physical hunger and spiritual emptiness, for example, can feel the same. Eating can interfere with an awareness of emotional cues.

I often visualize my mind as a rock tumbler. I toss an idea or word or feeling in and just let it roll around for a while until something tumbles forward and makes a connection.

If you want to know more about this technique, a similar approach is described in detail in the book *The Power of Focusing* by Ann Weiser Cornell, Ph.D.

So what did you discover? Which emotion — shame, guilt, or anger — is dominant for you? What do these sensations tell you about your internal belief system? What "truth" about yourself have you been avoiding looking at? Now that you can look at them in black and white on a piece of paper, which do you need to deal with, and which can you just let go?

Common Irrational Beliefs

The beliefs we uncover through the exercise of Internal Consultation are created in response to our own unique life experiences and family dynamics. Yet that doesn't mean that the beliefs themselves don't share common elements with the irrational beliefs of millions of others.

Cognitive Therapy is an approach to emotional healing that focuses on rewriting irrational beliefs. Here are some of the more common unhealthy beliefs that this school of psychology has identified. They are called Cognitive Distortions because they are not based on healthy reasoning:

I am worthless.
I must be loved by everyone, or I am not lovable.
I must do everything well, or I am incompetent.
I am the most stupid, untalented, or ugly person around.
I do not deserve to be happy unless I am perfect.
I do not deserve positive attention from others.
Other people's opinions of me are what matter most.
I am only valuable when I'm in a relationship.
Love is supposed to hurt.
If people pity me, it means they love me.
I should never burden others with my problems or fears.
I am powerless to solve my problems.
I must depend on others to keep my life on track.
I must NOT depend on others or ask for help; it is a sign of weakness.
No one cares about anyone else.
All men (or women) are dishonest, selfish, and/or close-minded.
If people are mean to me, they are horrible and unforgivable.
I will be happy only when everything is perfect.
There is only one right way of doing things.

There are always two choices: right or wrong; black or white; win or lose; pass or fail.

Admitting to a mistake or to failure is a sign of weakness.

The showing of any kind of emotion is wrong, and a sign of weakness.

My emotions are controlled by how other people treat me.

The world is a dangerous place, so I must be hyper-vigilant.

Most of us would not come straight out and say that we believe any of these things, but many of them sit just below our conscious awareness. That's why the Internal Consultation exercise is so helpful. If you felt a little "twinge" while reading any of these beliefs, you can take comfort in knowing that you are not alone. You might want to sit with them a while and see how strongly you identify with them, and think about how they might be shaping your actions.

Cognitive Therapy attempts to identify and then rewrite these beliefs. It works for many people and many beliefs. But I take issue with one aspect of their approach. They say that it doesn't matter where these irrational beliefs came from. They believe there is no need to explore your past and figure out who told you these things or what experiences led you to accept them. They say that all you need to do is identify the unhealthy belief and then rewrite it.

The problem I have with this is that these beliefs were often taught to us by people we love or who held positions of authority. Our conscious minds might be willing to accept that our therapist's beliefs are healthier than our inner voice's. But when our inner child hears our therapist contradicting our mother or father or preacher, or even our own experience, the therapist's opinion doesn't stand a chance. We will subconsciously sabotage our efforts to change our beliefs — even as we consciously claim to accept them. On the other hand, when we know where the beliefs came from, we can honor the source before gently reeducating our inner child.

One of my irrational beliefs, for example, was that in order to be a good artist, one must live a life of chaos. Artists are a little crazy. This is a notion that is perpetuated by society, but for me it had deeper roots. My sister was a naturally talented artist, but she was also schizophrenic and was unable to function as an artist.

It was my love for her that inspired me to become an artist like her, but along the way I also absorbed the idea that I would have to be a little crazy like her as well. Before I could accept the idea that I could be a sane, serene, successful artist, I had to honor my love for my sister while letting go of her example. If I didn't know how my belief was tied to my love for her, I might not have been able to let go of the belief while holding on to the love.

Shame

Forgiving others involves healing anger and resentment. Forgiving oneself involves healing shame.

While exploring what you believed were your core sins and uncovering your dysfunctional beliefs, you may have experienced waves of shame. "How could I have done that?" "How could I have believed that?" "How do I *stop* believing that?"

Shame is the sensation that we want to get away from when we say we want to forgive ourselves. Shame is the emotion that is often hiding behind our anger when we are irrationally triggered by someone's words or actions. Healing shame is some of the most important work we can do. Entire books have been written about it (I recommend John Bradshaw's *Healing the Shame that Binds*.) What I will offer you here is a brief overview and some insights on the underlying beliefs that help reinforce toxic shame.

What is Shame?

First of all, we need to know what healthy shame is. Shame is simply an emotional reaction to a flash of self-awareness in which we realize that we are not perfect, that we are, in fact, human. This is a good thing. Being human is a good thing. Knowing we are human is a good thing. Knowing that we are not perfect is a *very good thing*.

When we do anything, what we are really doing is making a choice. Most choices are rarely earth-shattering; they simply involve an attempt to balance competing goals. When added together over the course of our lives, however, these choices define who we are and create our legacy. When we feel guilt, it tells us that we know the decision we are *about to make* is not the best one possible. When we feel a twinge of shame, it is simply telling us that the decision *we just made* could have been better. This is a good thing, because it allows us to either change our decision or make a different one in the future.

Shame is like a little alarm that buzzes when we make a mistake. It lets us know that we need to adjust our behavior. Without it, we cannot recognize or learn from mistakes. We cannot become better.

Guilt is similar to shame, but it is the result of *knowing* that what you are about to do is unwise or unkind, but doing it anyway. Shame comes after the mistake. Guilt comes before, during, and after. Because both of these are generally unpleasant sensations, they motivate us to avoid shameful situations and making bad decisions.

So, if healthy shame is a good thing, how does it become unhealthy? Shame becomes toxic when we combine it with two cognitive distortions that affect the thinking of almost everyone in our culture. The first is perfectionism. The second is black-and-white thinking (also known as all-or-nothing thinking).

You see, our shame alarm is designed to sound only if the difference between our two choices is moderately significant. Like a smoke detector, it is designed to ignore household dust or even Chinese stir-fry cooking. It only sounds if we are in danger of doing something spiritually unhealthy.

If, however, we are perfectionists, then our internal alarm is set for zero tolerance. Because perfection is impossible, our shame response gets stuck in the "on" position permanently. We spend our lives thinking that nothing we do will ever be good enough.

It wouldn't be so bad to have our shame alarm ringing constantly if it were just a soft buzz, but that isn't what happens when we combine perfectionism with black-and-white thinking.

Black-and-white thinking — the belief that everything is either right or wrong, good or bad, saved or damned — locks our shame alarm on high volume. Making a mistake isn't just a mild annoyance, it means that we are damned to Hell, doomed to fail, worthless, and irredeemable. Even when we spend our days pretending that we are godly, there is always a part of us that knows that we aren't 100-percent right, so we secretly feel we must be 100-percent wrong.

The feeling that being imperfect is a fatal flaw is reinforced by our culture's dominant religious beliefs. Even if we are not raised Christian, belief in original sin and heaven and hell is infused into almost every aspect of our culture. As a result, we carry a saved/damned duality deep in our psyches. For centuries, Christianity has taught that we are in need of salvation and deserving of damnation. It has also described a stark, black-and-white division between the forces of good and the forces of evil. While the last few decades have seen a shift in some denominations, two-thousand years of perfectionism and damnation do not disappear from our collective world-view that easily.

The same church that tells us we are damned also tells us that we are forgiven – if we follow its rules. But even when we do so, intellectually *believing* we are forgiven and *feeling* forgiven are two very different things. When we feel unforgivable, we don't believe we deserve to be happy, so we continue to punish ourselves with constant criticism that feeds our guilt and shame.

> *Emotional abuse also comes in the form of rigidity, perfectionism, and control. Perfectionism produces a deep sense of toxic shame. No matter what you do, you never measure up. All shame-based families use perfectionism, control, and blame as manipulating rules. Nothing you say, do, feel, or think is okay. You shouldn't feel what you feel, your ideas are crazy, your desires are stupid. You are continuously found to be flawed and defective."* – John Bradshaw

"Shame unravels our connection to others. In fact, I often refer to shame as the fear of disconnection - the fear of being perceived as flawed and unworthy of acceptance or belonging.

Shame keeps us from telling our own stories and prevents us from listening to others tell their stories. We silence our voices and keep our secrets out of the fear of disconnection." — Brené Brown

Projecting Our Shame onto Others

The dangers of perfectionism and black-and-white thinking play out in a different way when we apply them to our relationship to others. When projected outwards, they become hyper-sensitivity and judgmentalism. These two attitudes keep us hurt and angry and make it d ifficult to forgive. When dealing with others, we also add a third unhelpful mindset, which is globalizing.

Just as it is good to be able to tell when we've made a mistake so we can correct it, it is good to be able to recognize when other people are doing things that are not in our best interest. We can't recognize kindness, for example, without also being able to recognize when people are rude. This is a good thing. Being able to discern exactly how kind or rude a person is on a scale from one to a hundred would be very useful. It would help you choose who to spend your time with and, even more important, it would help you identify what behaviors you should practice.

Here is where we get into trouble: if, on that scale from one to a hundred, we say, "I prefer to be around people between ninety-five and one-hundred," then we are projecting our perfectionism onto the people around us. We are being way too sensitive to imperfections and will constantly be disappointed by the normal humans who populate our lives.

When we project our black-or-white thinking onto others, we become judgmental, and cut people out of our lives for failing to meet our standards. "I refuse to be friends with someone who does ABC." Or, worse, "I will never forgive anyone who does XYZ."

When we combine the two, we set unrealistic standards for our friendships and then feel hurt, angry, or even vengeful towards anyone who doesn't meet them.

Finally, we can also globalize based on one flaw or one mistake. If a person fails to live up to one of our standards, we can project that failure onto them as an entire person, deciding that their one mistake is a reflection of their entire character.

When we do all three—have high expectations, have strong judgments against anyone who falls below them, and judge a person's entire character based on one failure—then we doom ourselves to being constantly angry at everyone. We have also placed our own serenity firmly in the hands of every stranger we meet...*every stranger we meet.*

What Does This Look Like?

How do we know if we are letting perfectionism, globalizing, and judgment affect our perceptions? If you look back at the list of irrational beliefs addressed in Cognitive Therapy, you will see several that are extensions of these three ways of seeing ourselves and others.

Do you find yourself using words like *awful, horrible, evil, worst, hate, unforgivable, insane, crazy, unbelievable, always,* and *never*? How about *best, perfect,* and *amazing*?

When we think of things in the extreme, we run the risk of catastrophizing our bad experiences and idealizing our good ones. This is another form of cognitive distortion. What we *need* to be doing is evaluating them objectively through discernment.

Using Discernment to Heal Shame

Discernment is the ability to evaluate our actions and the actions of others through an objective lens rather than through the lens of perfectionism and black-and-white thinking. It is the ability to see all of our choices in shades of gray, and a recognition that life is about making progress, not about arriving at some ideal destination.

Another way of thinking of it is that discernment is looking at the world through they eyes of a loving and patient God, not a God of wrath and vengeance.

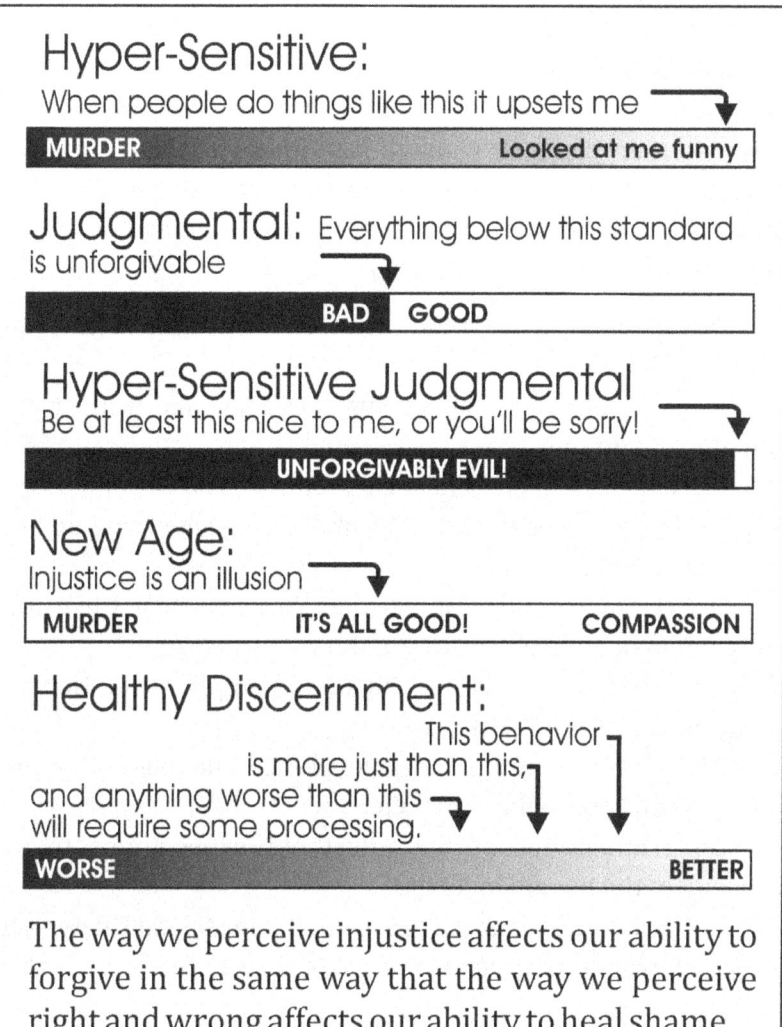

The way we perceive injustice affects our ability to forgive in the same way that the way we perceive right and wrong affects our ability to heal shame.

When we use discernment, we use moderate words like *unhelpful, unwise, unfortunate, hurtful, painful, worrying, immature, inappropriate,* and *dislike* for our difficult experiences. Our positive experiences are not perfect, but they can be *very good, enjoyable, appreciated*, and even *loved*.

Moving from perfectionism to discernment requires us to pay attention to the words we use both in our speech and in our thoughts. Try to catch yourself when you use extreme language and reframe the situation using more moderate words. How often do you hear yourself say "I *hate* it when..." or "this *always* happens to me...?" We often do this out of habit, but it is an accurate reflection of our perfectionist, judgmental, globalizing perspective on ourselves and others.

Discernment takes "I hate it when" and turns it into "I'm sorry this happened."

Discernment takes "he always does this," and turns it into "he tends to do this."

Discernment takes "I'm such a failure," and turns it into "I could have done better this time, and here's how I will do better tomorrow."

Discernment takes our big mistakes and puts them into the context of a life of learning and transformation.

Discernment takes our "sins" and applies the Hebrew definition of "missing the mark."

Discernment means we give people the benefit of the doubt when they make a mistake.

Discernment means we adjust our expectations to the capacity of the people involved.

Discernment means we are aware of our friend's flaws and make allowances for them as long as they don't become abusive.

By applying the idea of discernment to both our mistakes and those of the people who have hurt us, we will be able to reduce the amount of guilt and shame we feel towards ourselves, and to lessen the resentment we feel towards others by a considerably degree.

Forgiving Our Minor Transgressions

So far, the discussion about forgiving ourselves has focused on our negative beliefs about ourselves and the existential sins that we believed ourselves guilty of – most of which took place inside our imaginations. The more successful we are at addressing these big underlying issues, the easier it will be to feel good about ourselves, which will make forgiving our minor transgressions much easier.

All of us do things on a regular basis that we look back on later and think *I shouldn't have done that.* Some of us feel minor pangs of regret about these things. Others of us feel crushing guilt or shame over even the smallest of mistakes. Which category we fall into depends on how sensitive we are to mistakes and how judgmental we are about them. By being more aware of our perfectionism and applying the concept of discernment, we can move many of our "major" transgressions into the "minor" transgression column. The things we did are no longer evil, horrible, or unforgivable. They are now immature, unwise, and unfortunate, which makes them easier to forgive but not necessarily instantly forgiven.

Here are some simple tools you can use to relieve yourself of the guilt you feel for these minor transgressions.

The first is to simply ask yourself, *"How likely is it that the person I harmed remembers the event or thinks about it with pain?"* In other words, just because we've made a mistake or done something hurtful doesn't mean that we actually hurt the other person enough to matter. Realizing this can be a great relief and lift a heavy burden of guilt.

Another powerful exercise you can do in relation to minor offenses is to try to identify the virtue or character trait that you were failing to practice. This is a two-step process.

First, think about what you *wish* you had done instead of the thing you feel guilty about. Imagine for a moment that you were blessed with your current level of maturity and were given a "do over." What might you have said or done differently?

Now, think about what quality you would need in order to recognize and act upon this better response. Are you applying a greater level of kindness, patience, tact, empathy, or forgiveness? Do you now have more information or insight than you had at the time? Would you have needed more courage to do the right thing? Are you simply wiser and more mature?

By focusing on the virtue that was needed to improve the situation, you can interrupt the tendency to globalize. Instead of thinking *I was horrible in that situation,* you can think *I needed more of this one specific virtue.* The ability to imagine a better response means that you have *more* of that virtue now.

Developing the habit of looking for the needed virtue does more than help you forgive yourself; it also helps you recognize the virtues you need in any future situation. The solution to the situation you are remembering may be specific, but the virtues needed to find and apply that solution are universal. You can generalize this virtues-based solution to future situations. Reviewing your mistakes with this perspective will make you a better person.

Here is a simple little affirmation you can say whenever you are reminded of something you did that makes you feel guilty or ashamed:

I forgive myself. I needed more [insert virtue here]. I have more [...] now.

For example:

I forgive myself. I needed more compassion. I have more compassion now.

I forgive myself. I needed more patience. I have more patience now.

I forgive myself. I needed more self-restraint. I have more self-restraint now.

When you aren't sure what virtue was missing, you can always insert "wisdom" into the affirmation because wisdom is the virtue of knowing which virtue is needed in any given situation.

Likewise, you can do the same for other people's offenses. You can even modify the affirmations to help you forgive them.

For example:

I forgive you. You needed more compassion. I have enough compassion for both of us.

I forgive you. You needed more patience. I have enough patience for both of us.

Forgiving Our Major Transgressions

By exploring our faulty negative beliefs about ourselves and by practicing discernment rather than judgment, we've forgiven ourselves for a lot of normal human foibles. But what if there are still some big mistakes we've made that can't be let go of so easily? What if we have been mean, inconsiderate, selfish, and irresponsible, and it has caused real harm to ourselves and other people. How do we begin to forgive that?

It is said that hurt people hurt people.

The first step in understanding and forgiving your hurtful behavior is to look at it in the context of the pain, anger, hurt, and guilt that informed *all* of your decisions from early childhood on. When you make choices as to how to act, you are doing it based on who you believe you are. If you are given faulty information about who you are, then that will influence your choices. We also make choices based on how we believe the world works. If we were not taught the true meaning of love, the value of compassion, or the joys of practicing virtues, then those choices were not easily available to us. Forgiveness of anyone, including ourselves, requires a bit of compassion and understanding. We only know what we know. We can only give what we have to give.

Forgiving both ourselves and others involves reframing our experiences – looking at them from new, different, and more mature perspectives. We will explore the process of reframing in the next chapter.

When forgiving ourselves, however, there is an additional step that may need to be taken in order for us to truly rid ourselves of the emotional energy of self-blame and criticism. When letting go of perfectionism and judgment still leaves us with transgressions that we feel bad about, when putting our mistakes into the larger context of our own pain and struggle still doesn't absolve us of our responsibility for our harmful actions, there is a well-established system in place that is designed to help us let go of that last bit of negative energy.

It is called *Making Amends*.

If you know anything about twelve-step programs, you probably know that they encourage people to "make direct amends to all people we have harmed wherever possible, except when to do so would injure them or others." What you may not know is that it takes the first nine of the twelve steps to prepare for this process.

I'd like to share with you a modified version of steps four through nine and explain how they can be applied to forgiving ourselves.

#4. Made a searching and fearless moral inventory of ourselves.

A moral inventory includes both our strengths and our weaknesses – that is, which virtues we are good at and which we are not so good at.

An important thing to know about virtues is that any virtue taken to excess becomes a vice. That means we can also take any vice and study it to find the virtue hidden within it. The goal, then, is not to get rid of our bad qualities so much as it is to find a balance between competing virtues.

Courage, for example, is a virtue. So is prudence. Too much courage makes us foolhardy. Too much prudence makes us fearful. We need to find a balance.

As I wrote earlier, discernment is a virtue. Taken to an extreme, it becomes judgmental. It needs to be balanced with open-mindedness. But if you are too open-minded, you become gullible and have no standards.

Our moral inventory, then, invites us to take a hard look at which of our qualities are out of balance. If they are too far out of balance, then they have probably caused someone some harm along the way.

#5 Admitted to God, to ourselves, and to another human being, which of our qualities are out of balance and causing harm.

This is best done with a good therapist. It is a way to get objective feedback and shine a light on some of the areas of our life that have caused us shame. We can't change what we can't admit needs changing. Saying it out loud takes some of the mystery and power away from our mistakes.

#6 Were entirely ready to have God help us put our qualities into balance.

I haven't talked a lot about God's role in all of this, but God is the source of all of our virtues, so if we want to get them in balance, where better to turn than to the source?

#7 Humbly asked Him to bring our life into balance.

When it comes to forgiving ourselves, turning our weaknesses over to God is a powerful act. For many people, it has done more than anything else I describe in this book could ever do.

#8 Made a list of all persons we had harmed, and became willing to make amends to them all.

Taking our moral inventory in step 4 helps us look beyond any specific things we may have done wrong and points us towards patterns of behavior that have affected our relationships on a larger scale. That means that the list of people we have harmed may be more nuanced – and longer – than we might first suspect.

#9 Made direct amends to such people wherever possible, except when to do so would injure them or others, and made indirect amends to everyone else.

You may be under the impression that making amends to people is designed to make us feel ashamed and guilty. Actually, the result is just the opposite. It releases shame and guilt, and it breaks those sticky emotional bonds that keep us tied to our mistakes.

When we prepare to make amends, we are asked to acknowledge the pain we have caused others. This process invites us to feel compassion for them, to put ourselves in their shoes, and to imagine what our actions might have felt like from their perspective.

In other words, we aren't just saying, "I did this thing that I feel guilty about," we are asking, "How did this thing that I did affect you? What did it feel like? What was the nature of the wound I caused?"

This is a powerful exercise that gives us the opportunity to see ourselves through their eyes. We are voluntarily trying to see ourselves as abusers.

We may have spent much of our lives looking at other people as our abusers. Turning the mirror on ourselves can be transformative. Yes, it might make us temporarily feel worse about ourselves, but ultimately, it will help us feel compassion for the people we've hurt, for ourselves, and for the people who hurt us.

Hurt people hurt people. We were hurt by people who were hurt. Then we continued the cycle by hurting others. Abuse is a cycle. Understanding this does not excuse our behavior or theirs, but it does make it easier to forgive. The question of blame and the need to hate lose their power over us, as we wash them all away with the light of compassion.

Making amends is a profound and complex process. I don't expect or even advise that you set out to make direct amends to those you have harmed until you have done a lot of preparatory work. But you can begin making indirect amends immediately.

What do I mean by that? Direct amends means apologizing, paying back loans, returning stolen items, and doing specific things to make up for harm you may have caused someone. Attempting to do this before you have worked through a lot of healing could be like sending a bull into a china shop to apologize for a broken teacup. It could do more harm than good. Work with a therapist or a 12-step sponsor before setting out to do it.

Indirect amends, however, simply involve *being a better person* than you were before.

When you know that your virtues are out of balance, and you make sincere efforts to adjust, you are making amends. When you admit that you have hurt other people, stop hurting them. Be kinder. Be more compassionate. Be more supportive. Be more...forgiving.

If you've done something so bad that this kind of indirect amends doesn't seem like enough, then do something extra that relates to your earlier mistake. Donate money to a shelter. Volunteer as a big brother or sister. Join MADD and work to reduce drunk driving. Mentor someone.

As I said, anger tells us to act and gives us the energy to do so. Anger at ourselves can power guilt or it can power action. Doing *something* will help use up that energy in a productive and compassionate way.

The Payoff for Blame

And yet, after all of this – the deep introspection and the helpful tools – many of us still resist the idea of forgiveness.

Unless you have murdered someone or robbed a bank, why would you NOT want to forgive yourself for all of the minor transgressions that you've been feeling guilty about?

And if you think you HAVE forgiven yourself and have resolved the global issues that had convinced you that you were unworthy, then nothing anyone else has done to you can interfere with your well-being. Why wouldn't you forgive them?

In light of the fact that you are a good, noble, and deserving human being, what might be keeping you from letting go of your guilt, anger, and resentment?

Good questions, huh?

You see, there is a payoff for everything we do. Until we understand what we are subconsciously gaining from our guilt and resentment, we won't be willing to let go of it, no matter how much we believe we should and no matter how much we learn about how to do it.

For most of us, the payoff is simple: When we get hurt, we try to make sense of it by figuring out who is to blame. There is a difference between blame and responsibility. Responsibility is an obligation to act. Blame is an emotion. Strong emotions are a great distraction from constructive action.

If we think that WE are to blame, then we feel defeated, hopeless, helpless, worthless, and deserving of all of the bad things that happen to us. That sounds pretty bad, but as long as we focus on the emotion, we don't have to actually DO anything to change our lives. When given the choice between feeling helpless and taking positive action, our negative core beliefs and run-away perfectionism convince many of us that feeling bad is better than risking failure.

Others among us decide that it feels better to blame someone else. If we think that someone ELSE is to blame, then we can feel angry instead and focus on *their* faults instead of ours. If we blame others for what they did to us, we can wallow in both self-pity and resentment instead of taking action to restore our well-being.

This means that the payoff for not forgiving *ourselves* is that we don't have to take responsibility for actually correcting our mistakes, and the payoff for resenting *others* is that it keeps the blame focused outwards, making other people responsible for our happiness.

Anger and guilt are messengers. Anger says "ACT." Guilt says "CHANGE." As long as we are arm-wrestling the messengers, we don't have to do either.

When we love ourselves, we aren't afraid of taking responsibility for our actions because we know that we don't have to be perfect in order to be worthy. This means we don't have to blame or feel resentment towards anyone else either.

Loving Ourselves

Learning to love ourselves is simple, but it is not easy.

If we want to love ourselves, we need to become more loveable. To become more loveable, we need to develop lovable qualities.

It is that simple, and that hard.

Forgiveness is one of the most lovable qualities we can practice. Others include compassion, patience, generosity, gratitude, honesty, faith, and joy.

All of these qualities are already within us, so we are already lovable, but actually practicing them will make us even more so.

No matter how many hours you spend in front of a mirror saying "I'm lovable," it won't make you nearly as lovable as a single moment practicing one of these virtues in your interactions with others.

You can't love yourself while carrying around resentment for the people around you.

Your heart knows who you really are.

So which comes first, loving and forgiving ourselves, or becoming lovable?

Writing about self-love and forgiveness is a balancing act.

On one hand there are many people who grew up believing that life was a debt, not a gift – that they had to earn their place in the world by being perfect and never making a mistake. These people feel guilty for every plastic bag they failed to recycle and every thank-you card they failed to write. They feel shame over every answer they got wrong on every quiz and every relationship that ended badly. These people need to hear that they are wonderful, noble children of God, and they are loved and lovable exactly as they are.

On the other hand, some of us are mean. We insult our friends, laugh at other's misfortune, hold resentments for years, and refuse to take responsibility for the harm we cause others. We need to take a long hard look at our actions and make changes in our behavior. Forgiveness is not enough. We need to develop our virtues and make amends for the damage we have caused. We can't forgive and love ourselves until we truly do become more lovable. All of the loving slogans, rainbows, and unicorns people send us to make us feel good just feel like lies. We know they don't apply to us.

Strangely, these two groups of people can be comprised of exactly the same individuals.

Hurt people hurt people.

That's what we do, whether it is intentional or accidental.

So two things are true: We are wonderful, noble children of God who are lovable exactly the way we are, AND we need to change so that we have even more noble qualities to love.

That change can start when we learn to forgive others.

Forgiving Others

It is said that holding on to anger and resentment is like drinking poison and waiting for the other person to die.

I have compared resentment to scratching at a scab every day so that your wounds never heal. We might also say that focusing on our anger is like opening a wound in hopes that the other person will bleed. They are blissfully unaware of the pain you are inflicting on yourself.

Staying angry is painful. It can destroy our health and our relationships. It takes the joy out of life and makes us feel like victims.

So why do so many people cling to resentment?

I have offered two explanations so far. They may seem completely contradictory, and yet both can be true.

We can hold on to resentment because we were wounded, and we desperately need someone to validate our feelings and confirm our perception of reality. It is frightening to think that we are crazy, out of touch, or, worse, deserving of bad treatment.

We can also hold on to resentment because if we DO seek that validation and heal the wound, we would then be required to move on – to act, to change, and to let go of our victim mindset. Changing our reality is just as frightening as denying it.

As we move from focusing on forgiving ourselves to forgiving others, we will gain freedom from the pain that our anger causes. We will no longer be constantly opening up old wounds. That's a good thing. But we will also have to face the fear that comes from accepting the need to change. Letting go of anger changes our relationship to our past and our vision of our future. This is also a very good thing, but I would be lying if I pretended that it wasn't challenging.

"Forgiveness is giving up the hope that the past could have been any different." — Oprah Winfrey

The Short and Long Paths to Forgiving Others

Now that we've spend half of this book figuring out how to forgive ourselves, I can offer you two paths to forgiving others: the short path and the long path.

Notice that I didn't say the *easy* path and the *hard* path.

The short path is to focus on loving yourself and becoming the best person you possibly can be.

When you like yourself, nothing can emotionally hurt you. Nothing.

If you know you are a noble, worthy, confident, capable person, then nothing anyone says to you can hurt your feelings. Nothing they take away from you can change who you are. Nothing they do to you can wound your core reality.

The hurtful things they do are a reflection of them, not you.

When you know that – when you know it in the core of your being – then any injustice they send your way is simply an opportunity for you to respond with wise and compassionate action.

The flash of anger you experience when you recognize an injustice is just that – a flash. It immediately turns into an assessment of the situation and a decision to respond – or a willingness to turn it over to God and the universe.

When you love yourself, you always stand in the awareness that "hurt people hurt people" and you respond with compassion – even when compassion demands that you walk away or call the authorities.

The short path to forgiveness can be applied to past, present, and future injustices.

The short path is encapsulated in this series of affirmations:

I am innocent, why remain angry?
I create my own life, why blame others?
I am human; it is OK to make mistakes.
Even if it IS my fault, I still deserve to be happy and respected.
Anger is a Messenger, not a Commander.
Anger gives me energy for compassionate action.
What compassionate action will I use this energy for?

I'm a big fan of affirmations. Once we decide that we want to love ourselves and forgive others, we can solidify this new perspective in our subconscious by developing phrases that reinforce these goals and saying them several times a day. While giving yourself a daily pep-talk may sound silly, it is much less silly — and a whole lot less depressing —than continuing to listen to all of the negative self-talk and criticism that is currently bouncing around inside your head. You can go online to find more information about affirmations, or ask your therapist about how to use affirmations to shift your internal beliefs.

Here's the one I offered earlier. Now that you know more about yourself, it might be even more effective.

I forgive myself. I needed more ***. I have more *** now.

The Long Path to Forgiveness

Here is where we rejoin the rest of the world of forgiveness research. Most books and articles on forgiveness will focus on reducing your resistance to forgiving those who hurt you and reframing your experiences in order to make them easier to forgive.

Resistance to Forgiveness

Given all of the benefits of forgiveness, the short path to forgiveness would seem like the logical choice, and yet most people will not take it. I've offered two "payoffs" for holding on to resentment, but these are based in deep emotions. Most people will give more rational excuses for refusing to forgive.

Research shows that most of the reasons why people are afraid to forgive are based on mistaken ideas of what forgiveness really is. For example, people believe that to forgive someone means to absolve them from guilt. It doesn't. A person can legitimately be the meanest, nastiest person on earth, and you can still forgive them, while continuing to understand that they are the meanest, nastiest person on the planet.

> *"People have to forgive. We don't have to like them, we don't have to be friends with them, we don't have to send them hearts in text messages, but we have to forgive them.... Because if we don't we are tying rocks to our feet, too much for our wings to carry!"* — C. JoyBell C.

Forgiving is not forgetting. It does not give people permission to commit additional injustices. It is not being a patsy, wimp, or coward.

> *"Forgiving does not erase the bitter past. A healed memory is not a deleted memory. Instead, forgiving what we cannot forget creates a new way to remember. We change the memory of our past into a hope for our future."*
> — Lewis B. Smedes

Forgiveness does not let people off the hook. It only lets them off of *your* hook. People will still suffer the natural consequences of their own actions — it is just that you won't be keeping score. Will they "get away with it?" No. Their unjust action will follow them around for the rest of their lives and beyond. Don't let it do the same for you.

> *"Forgiveness has nothing to do with absolving a criminal of his crime. It has everything to do with relieving oneself of the burden of being a victim—letting go of the pain and transforming oneself from victim to survivor."* — C.R. Strahan

Some people believe that holding on to anger is a way to punish the person who hurt them, so they hold on to it as a form of revenge. Of course, anger hurts the person feeling the anger more than the one they are angry at, so it kind of backfires. Buddha is claimed to have said that holding on to anger is like picking up a hot coal with the intention of throwing it at someone else. You are the one who gets burned. Likewise, picking at your scab won't make the other person bleed.

Holding on to anger until someone apologizes is equally counterproductive. The anger creates tension; the tension creates distance. The distance makes it harder for the other person to apologize and increases the likelihood that they will find a way to feel as though they are the injured party.

Forgiveness is not reconciliation, which involves reestablishing a harmonious relationship with the person who hurt you. You can forgive someone and still choose to cut them out of your life as a form of self-protection. Sometimes reconciliation is appropriate, but it takes two people and a safe situation. Sometimes we have to forgive from a distance and even forgive people who still hate us and want to hurt us. That's their Karma. Ours is to let it go and move on to something better and brighter.

If we fear reconciliation, we have a right to listen to that fear, but we shouldn't let that get in the way of forgiveness.

If we long for reconciliation, we have a right to feel that longing, but if it is the motivation for forgiveness, it might just open another wound when it does not come.

So, if forgiving a person does not mean that you think their actions are appropriate, and it does not mean that you are willing to let them back into your life, what does it mean?

Forgiveness is letting go of the anger that keeps you emotionally chained to a person or event. Forgiveness means that you can stop thinking about the hurtful things that were done to you. Forgiveness means that you can think of the person or event without your heart racing or obsessive thoughts intruding on your serenity.

Forgiveness means that the person or event no longer colors your thinking or behavior as you move forward with your life.

It is a gift that you give, not to them, but to yourself.

Once you are free of the emotional charge associated with your anger towards this person, you may or may not find it comfortable to be with them. You may or may not decide that what they did was not as bad as you thought. Whatever you decide, it will be decided with a clear head and a clean heart.

Apologies, punishment, forgetting, reconciliation—these are all specific outcomes that we may cling to through our resentment. Because they are all outside of our control, clinging to them may leave us swimming in resentment for decades. Letting go of these expectations will free our energies for more productive pursuits.

Some Quotations about What Forgiveness Isn't

"Forgiveness isn't approving what happened. It's choosing to rise above it." —Robin Sharma

"But if you forgive someone for something they did to you, it doesn't mean you agree with what they did or believe it was right. Forgiving that person means you have chosen not to dwell on the matter anymore; you have moved on with your life." — Idowu Koyenikan

"The act of forgiveness takes place in our own mind. It really has nothing to do with the other person."
—Louise Hay

"We don't forgive people because they deserve it. We forgive them because they need it—because we need it."
— Bree Despain

"Sincere forgiveness isn't colored with expectations that the other person apologize or change. Don't worry whether or not they finally understand you. Love them and release them. Life feeds back truth to people in its own way and time." — Sara Paddison

"Forgiveness is a personal process that doesn't depend on us having direct contact with the people who have hurt us." — Sharon Salzberg

One Final Payoff

This will sound horrible, but it is true: anger and resentment release adrenaline and endorphins. These are drugs, and like many drugs, they can be addictive. Anger-fired adrenaline is better than a Starbuck's coffee to get you moving in the morning. A dopamine rush can be as euphoric as cocaine. If you enjoy getting angry, it will take extra effort to find the motivation to let go of the rush. But like other addictive drugs, the chemicals released by anger will take a toll on your body and ruin your health. *(See supplemental material about the physical cost of resentment at the end of this book.)*

"...it turns out that your brain on grievance looks a lot like your brain on drugs. In fact, brain imaging studies show that harboring a grievance (a perceived wrong or injustice, real or imagined) activates the same neural reward circuitry as narcotics. This isn't a metaphor; it's brain biology." — James Kimmel, Jr.

Reframing Your Experiences

"Reframing" is just psychologist lingo for looking at things from a different perspective. Our resentment – that emotional energy we associate with an injustice – is attached to a particular perspective. When we change our perspective, that cord of attachment can be broken more easily.

Reframing can actually take place on two different levels. We can reframe our *internal* experience by changing our perspective on the feelings we are having, and we can reframe the *external* experience by changing our perspective on the event that triggered our emotion or our view of the person involved. We can also change our perspective on what responses are available to us when we are feeling hurt.

The first thing we can reframe is our perspective on anger itself. If we believe that anger is a message from God telling us to attack the person who hurt us, then it will be much harder to forgive people than if we have a healthy understanding of anger.

We've already talked a lot about anger and resentment in general. Here is a quick review, and then we will move on to exploring them as it relates to specific events.

As I've said, anger is a sensation. It is *only* a sensation. It tells you that you have perceived an injustice in your life. Because justice is an important spiritual principle, anger is a very valuable tool for understanding your social environment.

BUT… anger doesn't tell you how big the injustice is. It doesn't tell you how accurate your perception is. It doesn't tell you what the other person's motivations were. It doesn't tell you what you should do about it. All it does is let you know that something doesn't feel fair.

Think of it like the smell of smoke. When you smell smoke, you don't throw your arms in the air and go running in circles screaming, "FIRE!" You use the information to guide you while you investigate your surroundings. The purpose of anger is not to get you all riled up and agitated. It is to give you useful information and the energy you need to act on it.

When that information and energy are used to fuel positive and compassionate action, then the messenger has served its purpose and goes away. You turn the smoke alarm off, the anger goes away, and you get on with your life.

But if no positive action is taken, then that energy gets stored away for later use and turns into resentment.

Resentment is an emotional investment in a specific outcome that is never achieved. Holding on to resentment is the result of feeling anger but not following through to positive action.

Forgiveness is a willingness to acknowledge anger, but let go of resentment.

To let go of resentment we have to work through the anger. Working through our anger towards *others* follows the same progression we talked about in relation to forgiving ourselves. First, you allow yourself to feel the feeling. Second, you recognize the source. Why are you angry? What triggered your emotional sensation? Where did this smoke come from?

As with your anger at yourself, the source of your anger towards others may include very old injustices that are difficult to name, as well as current or ongoing injustices in your daily life. In either case, you need to validate your right to be angry before you can begin to sort out the details of the specific injustice. Whether you are angry at your mother for not supporting you when you were young or at your spouse for not supporting you today, you need to accept that anger as valid in order to give yourself permission to explore just *how* valid the anger may or may not be.

Changing Our Perspective

Up until now, I have been defining anger as an emotional response to the absence of justice. While it is important for us to validate a feeling of anger as a legitimate response to a real injustice so that we can overcome the mental fog of resistance, fear and anger, once we have validated our feelings, it is time to turn on our rational minds and confess the obvious:

Anger is an emotional response to the *perceived* absence of justice.

In order to continue the process of resolving our anger we need to identify the specific injustice and choose an appropriate response. When we reach the stage of identifying the specific injustice that we want to resolve, we may discover that when the fog of resistance, fear, and anger are gone, it really *is not* an injustice. We may also come to realize that it *is*.

So, the next step is to assess our perception of the experience that has generated our feelings of anger.

Identify the Hurt

It may sound counter-intuitive, but one of the first things we can do *after* we have validated our anger is to ask whether it really is anger or not.

Remember, we are angry because we are hurt.

Consider this:

If someone were to run up to you, stab you in the chest with a knife, and run away, what would be the MOST important thing for you to do?

1) Identify the assailant.
2) Chase him down and stab him back.
3) Get to a hospital.

When we are angry, we get so caught up in assigning blame and getting revenge that we often skip the most important step, which is to identify the wound and treat it.

Many therapists call anger a "secondary emotion" because it comes *after* the emotion of being hurt. First you are wounded, then you decide that you didn't deserve to be wounded, and then you get angry. Getting angry is natural and healthy, but it is also a way of building a defense against being hurt again (or more). As I said many pages back, anger can be a wall to hide your hurt behind.

"Hurt" is a broad term that can mean anything from being stabbed by a knife to being hungry. So let's look at some of the emotions that can trigger anger:

Fear	Loneliness
Anxiety	Rejection
Frustration	Embarrassment
Confusion	Humiliation
Sadness	Stress
Isolation	Helplessness
Guilt	Exhaustion
Shame	Hunger
Jealousy	Chronic Pain

Some of these emotions are obvious triggers for anger, like humiliation or fear, but others are not so obvious. Have you ever tried to untangle a cord or ball of yarn and gotten so frustrated that you wanted to scream? It feels like anger, but there is no one to blame and no injustice to overcome. It is likely that when this happened you were also tired or stressed over something else.

If we understand that there might be other emotions – other hurts – hiding behind our anger, then after we tell ourselves that it is OK to be angry, we can take the next step and ask ourselves, "But what else might it be?"

Each of these painful emotions is just as legitimate as anger, and each of them can also be healed by compassionate intervention that has nothing to do with resentment.

If you find yourself getting angry at people who embarrass you in public, you can consider whether you need to work on being less embarrassed when you make mistakes, or you need to find new friends. In either case, the focus shifts from anger and blame to improving your interactions.

If you find you are angrier at the end of the day than at the beginning, perhaps what you need is an earlier bed time, not a new spouse.

If you are angry because you feel rejected, you can focus on rebuilding your relationship rather than lashing out with anger and blame.

If you pay attention to the emotions behind your anger, you will begin to see patterns. These patterns will very likely be reflections of the core issues you uncovered when working on self-forgiveness. This is why starting with self-forgiveness makes it so much easier to forgive others.

By reframing your internal experience and giving it a new name, you can become aware of many paths to healing that don't involve anger, blame, or resentment.

Of course, knowing the underlying emotion will not resolve all of your experiences of injustice. For example, if your anger is in response to fear because your safety is being threatened, understanding this will not solve the problem or remove the anger. It will, however give you clearer insights as to your path forward.

Each of these hidden emotions is a sign of a missing virtue or character strength that you need in order to heal. Naming them is the first step in finding their complement. If the preceding two sentences made no sense to you, see the supplemental material in the back of the book on healing through character strengths.

Is It Anger, Displaced Anger, or Rage?

Looking at the hurt emotions hiding behind our anger is one way of reframing our internal experience of anger. From there it is a short hop to understanding how two other kinds of emotion can hide behind a mask of normal anger. They are Displaced Anger and Rage. Understanding them can help us reframe our understanding of our most intense experiences of anger.

Displaced Anger

Displaced anger is when we are angry at one person or situation, but we project that anger onto someone or something else. There is a classic cartoon in four panels: In the first, a boss yells at a man. In the second, the man yells at his wife. The wife yells at her child, and the child kicks the dog. When I described this cartoon to a class of fifth-graders, they immediately understood the message. "So when my dad yells at me, he might not really be angry at me?" one kid asked. It broke my heart to hear the question, but the realization that he understood the idea gave me hope for his future.

We displace our anger most frequently when the cause of the injustice is more powerful than we are. To protest the injustices we receive from parents, teachers, clergy, bosses, bullies, police, or city hall would just invite additional punishment, and so we either express it towards someone even less powerful than we are, or we store it up as depression or rage.

Rage

The sensation of healthy anger is in proportion to the size of the injustice you are facing at this moment in time. The chemicals that shoot through your brain when you experience anger only last about 90 seconds. If your anger is overwhelming or builds over a long period of time, then it is probably rage.

Rage takes the injustice of the moment and throws it on the pile of every other injustice you have ever experienced, producing a raging fire of emotion. It is important to deal with the many injustices of your life, but it is impossible to deal with all of them at the same time. If you want to deal with one specific injustice, you will have to set the intense energy of rage aside to be dealt with later. Just knowing that it is possible to separate anger from rage can be a source of serenity and strength. It means that you can acknowledge the injustices of your past without wrestling with them every time something goes wrong. By dealing with one source of anger at a time, even deep and debilitating rage can be resolved and healed.

Revisiting Core Issues

Displaced anger and rage can both arise as a result of being triggered. Triggers are an artifact of unresolved core issue.

When we worked on forgiving ourselves, we looked at core issues that made us feel ashamed of who we are and angry at our mistakes. We came to see that much of what has worried us for years is truly absurd. We are not evil, worthless, or guilty of any major transgressions against humanity.

When we realize that we are not really evil, we start to wonder how we came to believe these bad things about ourselves in the first place. Some of these absurd beliefs are the result of childish thought processes, but some of them were taught to us by the people we grew up with. In many cases, we were *encouraged*, either directly or indirectly, to believe that there was something wrong with us.

If we think about this for very long, it just might make us angry. After all, who told us that we were sinful creatures who deserved to go to hell for eternal punishment? Who made us feel as though *nothing* we did was good enough? Who failed to rescue us from the bullies and abusers that made us feel dirty, or ugly, or helpless, or guilty? Often, it was the people who were supposed to be protecting us.

"Thus children, unlike concentration camp inmates, are confronted by a tormentor they love." – John Bradshaw

You see, while a part of us believed that we had a reason to feel guilty and needed to be forgiven, another part of us—sometimes stronger, sometimes beaten down—knew that we were innocent. *That* part of us is angry. *That* part recognizes the fact that we were treated unjustly and accused of wrongs we did not commit or could not control. *That* part knows that we were lied to about our nobility and our humanity and our essential goodness. That part has a right to be angry – but not at the people you deal with today.

If we are not aware of these sources of anger, then they will unconsciously spill over into the daily allotment of minor wounds, insults, and injustices – resulting in displaced expressions of anger, or even rage.

The more aware we are of these sources of anger, the more easily we can consciously separate them from the wounds we experience *today*.

Learning Your Triggers

A *trigger* is a word or situation that you are especially sensitive to because of unresolved core issues or unresolved trauma. Comments that would not upset a person without your experience can make you feel uncomfortable or angry. Situations that others would find rude or irritating can set you into rage or a panic attack.

What does that feel like? A mild trigger can just feel like a little adrenaline kick, and an anger response that is out of proportion to the offense. A strong trigger can resemble a panic attack, with a racing heart, tingling arms and flushed face, or it can prompt a shame response, with the blood leaving the face and arms, difficulty breathing, profuse sweating, trembling, and an irregular heart beat. It can actually feel like a heart attack. These physiological reactions make it almost impossible for us to think clearly or to respond calmly to what is happening.

With such extreme physical sensations to warn us that we have been triggered, one would think that we would all know exactly what our triggers are. But because most of us blame the person or situation for our reaction, few of us actually pay attention to the triggers themselves. We say, "They made me so mad," instead of "I reacted so intensely to that situation."

Learning to recognize the pattern of things that trigger you could very well be the most important thing you ever do. If you don't know your triggers, then your reactions to them can destroy your relationships and alienate you from everyone you know.

Knowing your triggers is the first step in healing them, and they *can* be healed.

Here are some common triggers:
1. Being criticized or underestimated
2. Rejection from an acquaintance or love interest
3. Having your ideas belittled, making you feel incompetent
4. Being interrupted, talked over, and made to feel unheard
5. Bullying of any kind, even if it is disguised as playful teasing
6. Being abandoned by someone you care about
7. Failure of any kind
8. Being lied to or betrayed
9. Having cherished beliefs or values challenged
10. Being treated unfairly in any way

You will notice that ALL of these things are irritating to most people. So what is the difference between being irritated and being triggered?

If someone were to say "that was a stupid idea," a person who knows that they are not stupid would focus on the word "idea" and look for a better idea.

A person who is slightly insecure about their intelligence might feel irritated at the comment and try to defend the idea.

A person who has a history of being shamed about their intelligence would hear this as a personal attack on their core self-worth. They would feel their heart start to race, and they would lose focus on everything except the feeling of having been attacked. Their response might very well be to attack the person who made the comment in return – perhaps quite loudly.

In extreme cases, the trigger might seem completely unrelated. For example, someone might mention that their spouse has a PhD. A normal response might be to ask in what field or to congratulate them. A person who feels that their intelligence is always being judged against other people might respond with: "So, they think they are smarter than everyone else?"

Such a comment would baffle the speaker who had no intention of being insulting, and yet an ugly exchange could take place anyway.

Triggers hook into our deepest fears and insecurities and drag them to the surface. Once that happens, rational thought is almost impossible, and anger or rage often follows.

People who have been abused can be triggered by a guy wearing a beard, a slammed door, a whistle, a dark hallway, the bark of a dog, the sight of a belt, the smell of alcohol, a bad joke, a bad haircut, a lost phone connection, getting lost, not knowing where their partner is, comments about appearance, comments about intelligence, anything to do with sexuality or gender, anything… anything… anything.

We all know the stories about soldiers having panic attacks at the sound of fireworks. Emotional trauma is just as real as battlefield trauma, and the situations that can remind us of them are as varied as the people who suffered them.

But it is not the firework's fault that the soldier panics; it is the trauma's fault.

Likewise, it is not the insult, the joke, the whistle, or the comment that has caused you to fly into a panic or a rage. It is the trauma. Blaming the person or the situation and getting angry at them will not help you heal the trauma. It will only deepen the wound.

Earlier I described the process "Internal Consultation" that can help you get in touch with emotions and core beliefs that might not be serving you well.

Getting triggered is like doing Internal Consultation on loudspeakers that the whole world can hear. Many people around you already know what your triggers are, and some of them may be using them on purpose to manipulate you. When YOU know what your triggers are, you can look behind them to see what negative beliefs you are carrying about yourself. Then you can transform your negative belief into a positive one and not be triggered anymore.

Once you realize that what you are experiencing is a trigger, the healing needed is not about forgiving the current irritation. Focusing on the current irritation is a distraction. Forgiving the current irritation should be fairly easy. It is similar to dealing with displaced anger: "Oh, now I see. I'm not really mad at you, I'm mad at the people or the situation that originally traumatized me or taught me that I was unworthy."

Getting to this point while you are in the middle of being triggered is, of course, not so easy. To help you deal with triggers when they happen, I've included a section on triggers in the supplemental material at the end of this book. There I describe a number of techniques you can use to deal with the immediate aftermath of being triggered and the panic attacks that often accompany it.

Five Steps towards Forgiveness

Whether it is today's wounds or yesterday's, the process of forgiveness is the same, but it is important to know which is which. When you have identified a single issue or source of injustice that you want to resolve – and you know whether it is a core wound or a current wound — then you are ready to take the next five steps.

When identifying specific injustices, choosing a response and taking positive action, you can ask yourself these five questions:

1) Are my perceptions accurate—would it still seem unjust from a different perspective?

2) Can I let go of my need to respond to this injustice? Is it more important to address the anger and blame or to focus on healing the underlying wound?

3) Can I find a way to look past the injustice and love the person behind it?

4) Is there anything reasonable and non-inflammatory I can do to correct the injustice?

5) Can I see something positive that came out of it?

Mentally Assessing Your Emotional Perceptions

As I said, anger is the result of a *perceived* injustice. Sometimes what we perceive is inaccurate. Sometimes what we perceive is colored by our beliefs, by immaturity, by lack of information, or lack of experience. There are many situations, for example, that would seem unfair to a child that, to an adult, would seem perfectly reasonable. As a child, you had a right to be angry, but when you remember this source of anger as an adult, you can understand it and therefore let go of the emotional charge.

There are also situations that adults experience that seem completely unfair from one perspective but are understandable when seen from a different perspective or when more information is available. For example, if you think someone has hung up the phone on you, this belief will color your perception. What a mean thing to do! If you later find out that their cell phone battery died, then anger can evaporate in an instant.

It is not what *happens* to us that makes us angry, it is our perception that someone has treated us unjustly. As we mature, we become better at distinguishing between intentional harm and accidents, between malicious intent and distracted thoughtlessness.

Acquiring the virtues of patience, compassion, flexibility, and objectivity can assist in this process and help to mitigate or eliminate anger through understanding. We may decide that what our parents did to us really wasn't so bad. That doesn't change the pain we felt at the time, but it does help us let go of the anger now. We may realize that our expectations in life were naturally immature as children, and they currently may be unreasonable as adults. We don't always get what we want, but that doesn't mean life is unfair.

Many of us live our lives feeling defensive for good reason. We have not been treated well. But this attitude can be counter-productive. If we already feel victimized or unworthy, then we live in a constant state of needing positive feedback from others. *Anything* less than that can feel like an attack, and it can keep us feeling resentful and angry. In this condition, even "have a nice day" can be perceived as an unjust imposition and really tick us off.

When *we know* that we are good, noble souls, however, it becomes easier to forgive the thousands of little slights we can encounter or perceive in a confused and distracted world. We don't take things so personally. It becomes easier to forgive.

Separating the injustice from the blame

I have said that anger is a natural response to injustice, but what is injustice, really?

Each of us is a noble child of God. We all deserve to receive kindness, respect and encouragement. We deserve safety, security, education, food, and shelter. We feel sad when the virtues of God are absent from our lives. We feel angry when those virtues are denied to us through the actions of another person.

In other words, we are *sad* when we feel that there is an absence of virtues in our lives, but we feel *angry* when we convince ourselves that it is someone else's fault. So anger is a two-step process: first the recognition that we aren't receiving the virtues that we deserve, and second, the blaming of someone else.

As children, we are relatively powerless, so if there is a lack of kindness, encouragement, security, or food, it probably is someone else's fault. The ability to recognize that you deserve these things is very important for your spiritual growth. The need to blame is *not* so important. When we understand that what we are feeling is the absence of the virtues we needed, we can begin to consider the fact that no one can give us something that they, themselves, do not already have. How does one blame one's parents for not passing on a set of qualities that they never received from their parents?

We are absolutely right to be angry. But what is the point of holding on to resentment? What positive outcome can we possibly imagine might be the result? At some point, we have to decide that healing the wound is more important than holding on to the anger and blame.

As adults, we have a great deal of control over the virtues in our lives. Anger tells us that someone may be trying to threaten our security, self-esteem, or other virtues, but in most situations, *we* are the ones who control whether or not they succeed. Someone may insult us, but *we* choose whether to let it affect our self-esteem. Someone may cut us off in traffic, but unless they actually cause an accident, it is *we* who decide whether to be distracted the rest of the drive home. Someone may leave the toilet seat up, but *we* can interpret that as a sign of forgetfulness or a sign of disrespect. The ability to recognize rudeness, recklessness, and forgetfulness is a valuable skill that anger helps us develop. The desire to blame, retaliate, or fume over these lapses is not so helpful.

Hurt People Hurt People

I've said this several times, but it bears repeating. No one intentionally hurts another person unless they, themselves, are hurting. For them to intentionally want to hurt you, they must already be hurting at least as much, if not more than you are.

Understanding this can make all the difference.

A story:

In my seventh-grade music class in the late 1960s, I sat beside a football player with anger management issues. I was a long-haired hippy freak, so I was fair game. Every day, when the teacher turned his back on the class, he would slug me in the arm – hard enough to hurt, but not hard enough to do any real damage. He knew I was a pacifist and wouldn't hit back. Instead, I told him that he must have a lot of anger inside, and if he needed to get it out by hitting someone, then better me than someone else.

Yes, I really did.

And yes, he continued to hit me.

Then one day I was in a record store when he walked up beside me. I was a bit worried what would happen without the classroom environment to protect me. But he started talking to me about music. The conversation progressed, and he ended up walking me home, telling me stories about his girlfriend and trying to wound the opposing team on the football field.

Somehow, we became good friends. He is now a high school art teacher, and he deals with angry teens every day by showing them compassion and teaching them other ways to express themselves.

When people try to wound you, it isn't about you.

Reviewing Reframing

The first of our five steps of forgiveness was:

1) Are my perceptions accurate—would it still seem unjust from a different perspective?

The tools we can use to reassess our perceptions include:

Looking at the experience from a different perspective – from the other person's perspective, from a more mature perspective, with more information, or with more empathy.

Separating our awareness of an injustice from our need to blame someone.

Using discernment rather than judgment (discussed earlier).

Remembering that hurt people hurt people. It isn't about us.

Once we have applied these tools, the original injustice that made us angry may seem so small that it no longer requires a response. The positive action that will release the energy of our resentment is to simply let go of any need for vindication, restitution, revenge, or apology.

We can then easily move through steps two and three:

2) Can I let go of my need to respond to this injustice and focus my energy on healing instead?

3) Can I find a way to look past the injustice and love the person behind it?

From this new perspective, we can see that the messenger was wrong, it was a misunderstanding, or the injustice was too small to be worth worrying about, or healing the wound is more important than assigning blame. Anger has been dismissed—with gratitude—but dismissed all the same.

But sometimes all of the reframing in the world will not make an injustice seem small or easily forgotten. Sometimes the messenger is right. There is a fire, and we need to take action.

Choosing a Response

Not all injustices are the result of misunderstandings or minor irritations. Sometimes situations really are significantly and painfully unjust. There is a lot of injustice in the world, and the chances are good that you've experienced your share. What do you do then?

You've probably heard of the Serenity Prayer:

"God grant me the serenity to accept the things I cannot change, the courage to change the things I can and the wisdom to know the difference." —Reinhold Niebuhr

I rewrote it a few years ago to be a little less passive. I felt that the word "accept" could suggest that the bad things we couldn't change might have been ordained by God rather than committed by unjust people. Forgiveness is much more empowering than acceptance.

"God grant me the strength to forgive the injustices I cannot mend, the courage to mend the injustices that I can, and the wisdom to know the difference."

Once we have determined that the specific injustice that caused our anger is real and significant, then it is time for step four: find a reasonable and non-inflammatory response.

Is there something you can do that would actually make the situation better for everyone? Often the answer is *No*, in which case you need to take a deep breath and move on to letting go and finding a way to forgive the person involved. But sometimes the answer is *yes*.

Often these are times when the injustice is ongoing. Taking action can protect us or someone else from physical, emotional, or spiritual harm.

Children don't have the resources to correct most unjust situations, but as adults we have an obligation to at least consider trying. Even if we can't fix an entire problem, we can make an effort. Helping even a little bit can give us a sense of power and accomplishment that reduces our anger. Shame and depression are often linked to feelings of powerlessness. It is amazing how even little efforts in the cause of justice can lift our spirits and discharge our anger.

We must be careful, though, that our efforts at correcting an injustice are not excuses for exacting revenge instead. Revenge is not about correcting a situation; it is about punishing a person by causing them harm. The desire for revenge is unhealthy for several reasons.

First, revenge does not resolve anger, it simply perpetuates the cycle of abuse. Healing an injustice is not about punishing the perpetrator, but about restoring the well-being of the victim, whether it is yourself or another. If the injustice is severe enough, then it is the job of the courts to punish.

Second, the desire for revenge actually increases our feelings of powerlessness. Protecting ourselves is something we have a fair amount of control over. In taking steps toward this, we can satisfy our need to respond and let go of resentment. However, if our goal is punishment, we are emotionally invested in a type of response that we have little legitimate control over. While we wait for the slow wheels of justice to turn, our resentment will fester and grow, making us angrier, feeling less in control of our lives.

Third, it is impossible to feel both compassion and revenge at the same time. Looking forward to someone else's suffering—even if they absolutely deserve it—is a form of spiritual poison.

Once you are sure you are motivated by a desire for justice and not revenge, then choose a course of action. This is best done in consultation with people who can look at the situation objectively and whom you trust. This might involve separating yourself from an abusive situation. It could involve consulting with a lawyer, or a police officer, or a supervisor at work. It could even involve calling your congressperson or local newspaper to raise awareness of a larger injustice. Taking constructive action is a way to use the energy of your anger so that it doesn't bounce around in your heart forever.

Putting Your Energy to Better Use

Perhaps you aren't quite ready to let go of your resentments. After all, anger is what gives many people the energy to get up in the morning. But resentment is an emotional investment in an outcome. What if you took all of that investment, all of that emotional energy, and directed it towards a different outcome—one that was still directly related to the injustice you suffered but was not about revenge, punishment, or even reconciliation?

If we find that there is nothing we can do for the specific situation that we faced or are facing, perhaps there are things we can do in a related area that can make us feel that we are helping to address a larger injustice than our own. Volunteering at shelters, doing educational work with children, becoming a mentor in a youth program or a sponsor in a twelve-step program can all be manifestations of the "courage to change the things I can."

The outcome we dedicate ourselves to can also be more personal. Injustice robs us of the opportunity to experience important virtues. An appropriate response would be to learn everything you can about the virtues that were denied you in the past and commit yourself to developing them to the fullest in the years ahead.

Were you told you weren't creative? Take an art class.
Were you told you were stupid? Go back to school.
Were you denied a promotion? Brush up your resume.
Did a relationship end badly? Go out and meet new people.

Every challenge we face in life is an opportunity to learn and grow. Anger is like a flashing red arrow pointing to the challenges in your life that you are being invited to learn from. Not everyone is blessed with such clear road signs on the path of spiritual growth. Use them.

Perhaps more clearly than anything else, anger tells us that our lives have been devoid of compassion. The best response to injustice is an effort to develop compassion—if not compassion for the people who hurt you, then perhaps for the many like them that you meet at twelve-step meetings, in your daily life, or when looking in the mirror. You are not the same as the people who hurt you, and for that you can be grateful. But we are all products of this harsh world. Developing compassion for others will help you feel it for yourself.

Asking for God's Help

Many situations are so far in the past or are so large that we have no appropriate way to respond to them. What do we do then?

When the injustice is real and there is nothing you can do about it, then you *could* stew in your anger forever and let it eat away at your faith and joy. But that wouldn't be very helpful. Instead, you could turn your need to respond over to God.

That doesn't mean that you pray to God that the guilty party be hit with a lightning bolt or sent to hell. It means that you allow your faith in a higher justice—in the karmic principle of *you reap what you sow*—to melt the chains of resentment that keep you attached to the one who wronged you.

The recovery community of twelve-step programs encourages people to "let go and let God." That one phrase has helped keep millions of people sane and sober. It is the *surest* way to let go of resentments and allow the peace and serenity of forgiveness to seep into our souls. Yet, for many people, it is also the hardest.

At first, the act of letting go might just be a grudging, "OK, I'll stop obsessing about this and let God handle it. God will make sure they reap what they sow."

But the deeper meaning of *you reap what you sow* is that if you sow true forgiveness and compassion and positive thoughts towards those who have hurt you (and yourself), that is what your life will be filled with. That is why the highest form of forgiveness is more than simply letting go of resentment, it is a stepping past the injustice and looking for the lost child of God who perpetrated it.

This is where experience in a twelve-step community or guided therapy group can be helpful.* It can give you the experience of loving and forgiving people who have made terrible mistakes in their lives, including ones that may have hurt others. It is easier to forgive strangers because what makes forgiveness difficult is not the size of the injustice, but the size of our emotional investment in responding to it. When we don't have personal resentments to get in the way, we can see the good person behind the unjust act or the hurtful mistake. That experience makes it easier for us to see the good in the people who have hurt us and have been unjust.

Pray for Those Who Hurt You

One of the ways we know that all of the major religions come from somewhere greater than ourselves is that they tell us things we don't want to hear.

One of the most challenging statements in all of religion comes from Luke 6:27-36:

---

* *As in anything, there are good and bad twelve-step meetings and therapy groups. Find one that supports your growth, not your problems.*

But I say unto you which hear, Love your enemies, do good to them which hate you, Bless them that curse you, and **pray for them which despitefully use you.** *And unto him that smiteth thee on the one cheek offer also the other; and him that taketh away thy cloak forbid not to take thy coat also. Give to every man that asketh of thee; and of him that taketh away thy goods ask them not again.*

And as ye would that men should do to you, do ye also to them likewise. For if ye love them which love you, what thank have ye? for sinners also love those that love them. And if ye do good to them which do good to you, what thank have ye? for sinners also do even the same. And if ye lend to them of whom ye hope to receive, what thank have ye? for sinners also lend to sinners, to receive as much again. But love ye your enemies, and do good, and lend, hoping for nothing again; and your reward shall be great, and ye shall be the children of the Highest: for he is kind unto the unthankful and to the evil.

Be ye therefore merciful, as your Father also is merciful.

This might sound completely crazy, but one of the best ways to free ourselves of the negative energy around a person or situation is to pray for the spiritual growth of the person who hurt us. Anger is like a chain that ties us to the other person. Praying for them and "holding them in the light" is like handing that chain over to God. Praying for their forgiveness and growth helps us see them through God's eyes – as wounded children in need of healing.

The Alcoholics Anonymous *Big Book* puts it beautifully:

"If you have resentment you want to be free of, if you will pray for the person or thing that you resent, you will be free. If you will ask in prayer for everything you want for yourself to be given to them, you will be free. Ask for their

health, their prosperity, their happiness, and you will be free. Even when you don't really want it for them and your prayers are only words and you don't mean it, go ahead and do it anyway. Do it everyday for two weeks, and you will find you have come to mean it and to want it for them, and you will realize that where you used to feel bitterness and resentment and hatred, you now feel compassionate, understanding and love."

Prayer also serves the purpose of reminding us that we have a relationship to something that transcends anger, injustice, and whatever challenges we face today. We are connected to something eternal. Nothing that anyone does to us can change who we truly are.

Prayer is the simplest and most effective response we could ever possibly have. It can be used for every single injustice, and it can be used immediately or years later. You will find prayers for forgiveness, healing, and serenity in the back of this book.

Looking for the Gift

People hate this part because it forces them to admit that, as bad as the experience might have been, some good could still come out of it.

Here's the thing: we were not put here on this earth just to float through life twiddling our thumbs and watching Netflix. We are here to learn and grow. We are here to develop our inner strengths and become better people.

None of that is possible if we don't face challenges in life. We can't learn patience if we never have to wait. We can't learn compassion if we never witness suffering. We can't develop our talents if we are afraid of making mistakes, and we can't learn forgiveness unless someone does us wrong.

If you didn't give up when something bad happened, then you developed strength, perseverance, and, ultimately, more self-confidence. Don't minimize or belittle this accomplishment. Every time you forgive, rise above, and move forward in service, you become a better person.

The best and the worst thing that ever happened to me was that I spent seven years in a soul-crushing marriage. I honestly thank God for that experience because it forced me to hit bottom. From there, I went, kicking and screaming, into therapy. That's where I learned a lot of this wonderful stuff about forgiveness and compassion. (If you still aren't sure about this idea, you might want to pick up my book *Why Me? A Spiritual Guide to Growing Through Tests*.)

> "True forgiveness is when you can say, 'Thank you for that experience.'" — Oprah Winfrey

The Payoff for Compassionate Forgiveness

One of the side benefits of developing this capacity for forgiveness is that we can then apply it to our other tools for resolving anger. An attitude of compassionate forgiveness provides us with a new perspective on our old hurts. It is easier to see things from another person's point of view if we have already forgiven them and are giving them the benefit of the doubt.

Likewise, compassionate forgiveness makes it easier to rectify unjust situations because we approach them in a more loving, non-confrontational manner. We look for win-win solutions to problems rather than exacting revenge on those who may have hurt us in the past.

Validating the Letting Go

We are coming to the end of the process, so if you are still finding yourself resisting the idea of forgiveness, I will repeat here what I said at the beginning.

I think our deepest fear is that if we forgive someone, what we are really doing is ignoring the injustice, and that by doing that we are saying that the injustice was not real, it did not matter, or that it was not really an injustice at all.

Our fear is that to forgive is to accept that we deserved what happened to us.

To overcome that fear, we need to have our feelings validated. But even more than that, we need to have our entire process of forgiveness validated.

We *began* the process of dealing with our anger by validating the legitimacy of our *feelings*—confirming to ourselves and the world that we *didn't* deserve what happened to us. Now that we have looked at our experiences from different perspectives and explored different possible responses—including understanding and compassion—we can remove our final barriers to forgiveness by validating our *understanding* of our experience at the end of the process. This validation encompasses our feelings, our interpretation of the injustice, the response we have chosen and the actions we are taking.

We need to be heard – from beginning to end.

> *"Being heard is so close to being loved that for the average person, they are almost indistinguishable."*
> — David W. Augsburger

> *"The most basic of all human needs is the need to understand and be understood. The best way to understand people is to listen to them."* — Ralph G. Nichols

> *"If we can share our story with someone who responds with empathy and understanding, shame can't survive."*
> — Brené Brown

Once again, I encourage you to talk to a therapist or, share with a twelve-step group, or at least have a gripe session with a close friend *before* your final effort to let go of anger and resentment. You need to hear someone say—in words or with their silent encouragement, *"I'm so sorry that happened to you. You did not deserve to be treated that way."*

This *external validation* can go a long way in helping you get rid of anger and resentment.

This is where I believe a good therapist is better suited to help than friends or recovery groups because a therapist can both be objective and say *the words you need to hear.*

A therapist can help you through the steps of processing anger. They can help you determine if what you experienced was an injustice or if you need to change your perspective. They can help you find a safe and reasonable course of action to take. They can listen to you describe the injustice and help you name it so that you can let it go.

At the beginning, we needed to hear: *"Your emotions are valid."* At the end of the process, we need to hear: *"Your emotions were valid. Your interpretation of the experience makes sense. Your compassion for the people who hurt you is noble. Your chosen response is productive and appropriate. Your decision to forgive is well-grounded."*

Friends are not objective, and they may try to take sides or give advice on how to get revenge. In twelve-step groups, people don't generally speak directly to one another after sharing—though you can often see compassion and empathy in their eyes.

Serious injustices, though—especially ones that you dig up from your past—really require an objective witness who can verbalize the legitimacy of your pain. That's why a good therapist can remove one of the biggest obstacles to forgiveness. You can let go of the anger because it has been made real. It exists outside of your inner world because someone else has perceived the injustice and named it as such.

In fact, a therapist can often give the injustice an actual name. You might be surprised how healing this can be. Yes, that is *emotional abuse*. Yes, that is *spiritual abuse*. Yes, that is *sexual abuse*. Yes, that was *controlling and manipulative*. Yes, that was *abandonment*. Yes, the threat of violence is still *violence*. Yes, you were right to be frightened and angry for being treated that way. Yes, you can forgive this, even though it was an injustice. That is what forgiveness means.

Can it really be this easy? Sometimes, yes.

Again, resentment is an emotional investment in an outcome. Sometimes, sincere validation is the only outcome that you really need. Wrestling with your fears and anger, betraying family secrets, asking for help, these are the hard parts. Once your pain is validated, forgiveness and letting go often come easily.

> *"When I have been listened to and when I have been heard, I am able to re-perceive my world in a new way and to go on. It is astonishing how elements that seem insoluble become soluble when someone listens, how confusions that seem irremediable turn into relatively clear flowing streams when one is heard. I have deeply appreciated the times that I have experienced this sensitive, empathic, concentrated listening."* — Carl R. Rogers

> *"When we listen, we hear someone into existence."*
> — Laurie Buchanan, PhD

> *The beauty of listening is that, those who are listened to start feeling accepted, start taking their words more seriously and discovering their own true selves. Listening is a form of spiritual hospitality by which you invite strangers to become friends, to get to know their inner selves more fully, and even to dare to be silent with you."* — Henri J.M. Nouwen

Twelve Ways to Forgive

This has been a long and winding path to present the many and varied tools you can use to forgive others. Now that we are almost at the end, let me summarize them in a more concise way. Here are the many ways you can learn to forgive. You can use them individually or in combination, depending on the person or situation you are forgiving.

1) Love yourself enough that the other person's actions, comments, or opinions no longer matter to you.

2) Find someone to whom you matter, who can validate your feelings and soothe your pain – that is, someone to *"kiss it and make it feel better."*

3) Gain a more mature perspective on the event and realize that it wasn't intended to be hurtful at all.

4) Decide that however real the injustice, your energy is better spent focused on healing rather than assigning blame and taking revenge.

5) Realize that the anger you felt was the result of being triggered, and the person who triggered you was probably not intentionally at fault.

6) Without the mind-fog of shame, guilt, or anger, recognize your own part in the conflict, and stop blaming the other person.

7) Remember that hurt people hurt people and gain a more empathetic perspective on the actions of the person who hurt you.

8) Focus on restorative justice rather than revenge – taking constructive action to protect yourself and others against future injustices.

9) Redirect the energy of resentment into positive action focused on healing and service.

10) Pray for the person who hurt you.

11) Ask God to remove your resentments so you can forgive others as you have been forgiven.

12) Acknowledge the strengths gained and lessons learned because of the injustices you've experienced, and be grateful that they have made you a better person, who finds it easier to love themselves.

An Exercise:

This is not a workbook, so I haven't given you a bunch of worksheets and exercises to do. But now that we are nearing the end, it is time to see if you can put all of these ideas into practice.

Write down the names of six people (other than yourself) whom you would like to be able to forgive.

Which of the twelve ways to forgive will you make an effort to apply to each of them?

How do we know when we have succeeded in forgiving?

As I said when describing people's misunderstandings about forgiveness, forgiving does not mean that you like, trust, or want to spend time with the person who hurt you. It doesn't mean that you have forgotten what has happened or will make yourself vulnerable to future injustices. All it means is that you are no longer emotionally invested in the injustice. You are no longer interested in "looking under the Band-Aid." Thinking about the person or the event does not give you a twinge of anxiety, a rush of adrenaline, or an elevated heart rate. You no longer dwell on the event or relive it in your mind. You do not feel the need to respond to the person or event in word or deed, nor do you feel the need to avoid thinking about them. Your emotional serenity no longer has anything to do with that particular situation.

In short, it feels like your inner wound has been kissed by God. The scar is still there, but it no longer hurts.

It is a great feeling.

Supplemental Material

Training your Friends

Having explained why I strongly encourage you to find a good therapist, I also recognize that not all of us can afford a therapist, and that sometimes we face situations that we need to process right away. Waiting a week for a therapist's help might be too late.

Sometimes, you need to turn to a friend.

When we are hurt, our core need is to have our pain validated and to know that our pain matters to someone.

The need to matter – for our pain to matter and our life to matter to something outside of ourselves – is a core need, written into our spiritual DNA.

Who does your pain matter to?

I know that can be a very painful question, but creating an answer to that question might be the most important thing you get out of this book.

Sharing your experience with someone to whom you do not matter might be worse than not sharing it at all. In that case, *I encourage you to turn to a Higher Power*. If you believe in God, then turn to God. If you don't, then the 12-Step program encourages you to turn to anything bigger than yourself – the universe, nature, the moon and stars, the future, your cat, the song inside your head, your favorite book or poem, even your journal – whatever thing outside of yourself you can turn to with trust and a little awe. Find someone or something that you can matter to in the great scheme of life, and turn to it or them when you need support.

When you share with your friend, spouse (or even your chosen Higher Power), don't just unload on them and expect them to listen and respond the way you need them to. In our culture, we tend to try to "fix" things and give them advice. The LAST thing in the world you need when sharing a story about something someone did to you that made you mad is for them to tell you what you SHOULD have done. That just piles shame on top of anger.

Assuming that you are at the beginning of the process and are still living in your emotions, this is how you start:

> *I'm upset about something that has nothing to do with you.*
>
> *I need you to listen to what happened to me without giving me advice or telling me what I should have done differently. Can you do that? Thank you.*
>
> *When I'm done, I need you to tell me that you are sorry that this happened to me, that I didn't deserve it, and that I have a right to be angry.*
>
> *Then I need you to tell me that you have faith in me and that everything will be OK.*

After you've told your story, if they have responded as you asked, and if it is safe and appropriate, ask for a hug.

If you've shared with a Higher Power instead of a person, then don't demand answers or a fix. Just sit with it and imagine it smiling and nodding and saying all of the things you need to hear.

If you are needing validation at the *end* of your process, your request will be slightly different.

At the beginning, you needed to hear *"your emotions are valid."* At the end of the process, you need to hear your friend say:

Your emotions were valid.
Your interpretation of the experience makes sense.
Your compassion for the people who hurt you is noble.
Your chosen response is productive and appropriate.
Your decision to forgive is well-grounded.

Keep in mind that your friend doesn't need to believe that everything you've felt, said, or done is perfect, or even the best possible – only that it is valid. At the same time, give your friend permission to question your actions if they sincerely fear that they will be a danger to you or others. Even therapists stop us from causing ourselves harm.

Dealing with Triggers

This book has been about forgiveness, which means it is mostly about dealing with anger over things that happened in the past.

But what do we do with things that make us angry right here and now? Wouldn't it be nice to be able to process our anger in real time so that we don't have to carry it around to be forgiven later?

I will assume that by this point, you want to be forgiving and you understand the value of empathy, compassion, and reframing when a person or situation irritates you. These give you the tools you need for dealing with day-to-day petty injustices. But they may not be enough to keep you from being triggered by things that bring up past wounds. Yes, you have explored your unhealthy negative beliefs about yourself, and you are beginning to love yourself more, but none of us is perfect. We can all be triggered by something. So how do we deal with our emotions when they go ballistic?

Here is a quick course in anger management that addresses triggers and the panic attacks that can often follow as a result.

#1 Know Your Triggers, Know Your Triggers, Know Your Triggers

Let's start by being preemptive.

Write down every time in the last six months that you can remember getting angrier than the situation warranted and try to remember exactly what words were said, or what was done, that started the melt down. You may remember lots of them, but you might not remember them at all. That's because when you are triggered, your brain stops working. The next day – or even five minutes later – you might not be able to remember what was said or done to set you off.

This is such a universal phenomenon that many fights between couples consist of one trigger sparking the other person's trigger, followed by several hours of arguing over how the fight started. Neither can remember the exact word or action that set them off, but they are sure that they were being completely reasonable until the other person overreacted.

Scary, isn't it?

If you do remember these triggering moments, **write them down**, then try to find the patterns. What part of your self-esteem or security was being threatened?

If you can't remember enough initial triggers to be able to find any patterns, that's OK.

Starting today, **write down** every single thing that makes you angry – not so you can dwell on it, but so you can look for patterns. When you figure out what insecurity or fear was hiding behind the anger, *cross out* the description of the situation that made you angry, and write the name of the trigger instead.

With this list of triggers in mind, you can begin the process of healing the insecurities and fears that feed your anger. Work with a therapist or a journal to re-educate your inner child.

In the mean time, when you start to feel yourself being triggered, you can recognize the trigger and defuse it somewhat. Telling yourself that it is what happened to you as a child, not what is happening now, that is upsetting you can make it easier to process your anger and forgive the situation.

But "easier" does not mean that you won't still get upset or angry. Even when you know your triggers and are working on healing them, it is helpful to have a whole bag of anger management tricks at your disposal.

Here are just a few.

20 Anger Management Tricks

#1A was "know your triggers."

#1B is "know your partner's triggers." A little bit of objective research into this could save most relationships that are otherwise doomed to destruction.

#1C is "learn to recognize when friends, family, and strangers are *being* triggered." If you can recognize the fact that *they* are being triggered, then you are less likely to react badly when they say or do something that would normally trigger *you*.

#2 Whether it is you, your partner, or an acquaintance, the second trick to apply when someone is triggered is to simply **STOP**. Almost any *productive, useful, or healthy* response to an unjust situation can wait at least an hour, and probably a day or two. There are lots of *unhelpful* responses you can do immediately, but they are, well, *unhelpful*. They are unlikely to remedy the injustice and could very well cause physical, emotional or financial harm to you or others. It just isn't worth it.

#3A Take a deep breath, and count to ten, or fifty, or one-hundred – whatever it takes to calm that 90-second adrenaline rush that is a natural, healthy response to a perceived injustice.

#3B Close your eyes. You can do this while you take your deep breath and count. It creates a barrier between you and the situation – even if that barrier is only your eye lids. You can imagine yourself somewhere else, or imagine them gone. You can do this instead of physically leaving the situation, or you can do it in preparation for leaving.

#4 Memorize this magical phrase: **"Excuse me, I have to use the bathroom."** Saying this when you or someone else has been triggered will allow you to escape almost any social interaction within seconds. It might raise an eyebrow, but that is better than raising your voice.

Leaving a triggering situation is often the very best response. That doesn't mean that you pretend it never happened, because you will want to process it. But it does mean that you will be able to process it in your own time and on your own terms.

The genius of this phrase is that if the other person is triggered by abandonment, it won't freak them out. Even if you stay in the bathroom for three hours, they know where you are. Another advantage is that a warm bath or a cold shower is a great way to either comfort or distract you from your intense feelings. Yet another is that you can lock the door (or stall) and be somewhat protected if the other person's feelings escalate.

If you are in a social setting, and not dealing with a partner you will want to reconcile with later, you can also just head towards the bathroom and keep on going. You do not owe people you are not in a committed relationship with an explanation for why you left a triggering situation. This is also true if your partner is prone to violence when triggered. Just leave. *Abandonment issues be damned.*

The final benefit of this magical phrase is that it gives you the space you need to use some of the many other tricks that will help you calm down. After you have stopped and taken a deep breath, you might not want to start singing or meditating in front of the person who just triggered you.

Happiness Triggers: The above tools are designed to get you out of a triggering situation. Once you have escaped, you can try applying a "Happiness Trigger." These are similar to anger triggers except they generate a dopamine or serotonin response instead of an adrenaline response.

#5 Do some mild physical activity. Pass the bathroom by and go for a long walk outside in the fresh air and sunshine. Roll your head. Stretch. Do some muscle relaxation exercises. This will burn off adrenaline, get you out of your head and back into your body, and help you relax.

#6 The experts suggest that you play some music you like. I would go further and say crank up some upbeat tunes and sing at the top of your lungs, or clear your living room floor and do some serious dancing. You can also crank up some "angry" tunes and blast away. Expressing your anger through music in a safe environment can be healing on many levels. They also say that singin' the Blues makes you happy. Give it a try.

#7 Laugh. This is almost as good as singing and dancing, but it might be harder to do on command. Watch your favorite funny movie to help you calm down. Read a funny book or an online comic strip.

#8 Activate your senses. When you are freaked out or angry, your brain and your body are both running out of control. There is an exercise that can help get you back in control of your body.

Look at 5 separate objects. Think about each one for a short while.

Listen for 4 distinct sounds. Think about where they came from and what sets them apart.

Touch 3 objects. Consider their texture, temperature, and what their uses are.

Identify 2 different smells. This could be the smell of your coffee, your soap, or the laundry detergent on your clothes.

Name 1 thing you can taste. Notice whatever taste is in your mouth, or try tasting a piece of candy.

Other ways to activate your senses are to rock back and forth, rub a worry stone, wrap yourself in a fluffy blanket or sweater, squeeze a teddy bear, or take the above-mentioned hot bath or cold shower. Some people find that smelling lavender can be calming. Listening to white noise can keep your auditory nerves active and distracted.

Examples of other sensory happiness triggers are a favorite smell, a favorite meal, hot coffee or tea, and even clean sheets.

#9 Say an affirmation 100 times. Use one I've mentioned in this book, like "I am innocent, why stay angry?" or use your favorite. If you don't have a favorite, make one up. I'm a strong believer in the power of affirmations to help us rewrite the negative self-talk that goes through our head during the day. They are especially helpful as an anchor when we are triggered.

#10 Go to a "happy place" that you have created for yourself – a place that you have visualized in your mind, like a beach, a favorite room, spot in nature, or a Holy Place. This is a kind of visual affirmation in your head that visually-oriented people can use to center themselves. This is not something you can do on the spot. You need to have spent time creating this safe inner space in advance. Once you have built it and spent time there, you can step into it at a moment's notice when you need to.

#11 Meditate. This is similar to repeating an affirmation, but instead of trying to get our minds to focus on something positive, it is trying to clear the mind entirely. An affirmation can be seen as a way to resist the negative thoughts running through your head. Sometimes resistance just keeps the thoughts present. When that happens, meditating with a mantra can help wipe the slate clean and clear our heads.

When I was sixteen, I paid money to learn a popular meditation technique. I will tell you everything you need to know in the next few sentences for free. Ready? Choose an innocuous word, like "one" or "circle" that doesn't have any emotional significance for you, or make up a word that sounds nice to you with nonsense syllables. Sit quietly and comfortably. Close your eyes. Breathe naturally, and repeat the sound in your head for 10-20 minutes. That's it. If your thoughts drift off of your sound, gently bring them back.

Research has shown that this simple technique offers the same physiological and emotional benefits as the meditation you pay money for or go on expensive retreats to learn.

If this style of meditation doesn't work for you, there are literally hundreds of styles of meditation you can try, including online guided meditations and podcasts to help you relax.

#12 Combine #6, #8, #10 &#11. If something has upset you so much that you are having obsessive thoughts that just won't go away, distracting one part of your mind is not enough. Most of us have layers of thoughts, so even when we are trying to meditate or to say our affirmations, we can have stressful thoughts running in the background.

Try saying an affirmation or mantra while humming an "earworm" (a short tune that sticks in your head) while listening to white noise like a fan or waves crashing, while relaxing in your "happy place," while caressing a teddy bear or soft blanket.

This may sound extreme, but for some of us with multiple voices in our head, it is very useful. For other people, one calming mantra is all they need.

***

The first twelve anger management tools were just about getting you out of that initial intense feeling that comes from rage or being triggered. The following ones assume that you are somewhat calm. If you aren't, go back and try some more of the above tools.

#13 Write in a journal. Writing in a journal is an important way to learn about yourself and to release a lot of pain and anger.

When I had you do Internal Consultation, I told you to write down what you learned by talking with your feelings. I said that putting your negative beliefs down on paper could make huge, overwhelming fears and anxieties look small, manageable, and even silly. The same is true of resentments. Once they are down on paper, a lot of them look childish or insignificant.

Journals are not for anyone else. Write for yourself without filters and without judgment. Write what happened. Write how it feels. Write what you wish you had said. Write what you wish they had said. Write what it reminds you of in your past. Write what you fear it will mean in the future. Write it all down. This is how you learn your triggers, see your patterns, and watch yourself grow.

#14 Talk to a friend. This goes without saying, but I'll say it again here anyway. Review the section on training your friends, then allow them to care about you.

#15 Ask for a hug. Sometimes this works as well or better than talking.

#16 Attempt to practice empathy. Remember that if you can be triggered and react badly, other people can too. Hurt people hurt people. Review that section above, and then…

#17 Imagine forgiving them. That's it. Try to imagine the possibility of forgiveness. If this book has shown you the possibility of forgiving someone, then it is just a matter of time before you achieve it.

#18 Say or do something kind for someone. This gets your head away from focusing on yourself and your feelings and onto caring for others and practicing virtues.

#19 Find a creative outlet. Creativity is a wonderful way to fill the empty space left when you let go of anger and resentment. You have all of that invested energy that never got expressed in revenge. Use it for something constructive and creative. You might be amazed at what you produce.

> *"Creativity overcomes violation and is the answer to violence."* – John Bradshaw

#20 Practice gratitude.
Wait! What? Where did that come from?

You can't *get rid* of a bad belief or behavior. You have to *replace* it with something good. You replace anger and resentment with gratitude. Many people have found that writing down three things that they are grateful for at the end of each day can radically transform their lives. Just as you can't be angry and compassionate at the same time, you can't be resentful and thankful at the same time.

Forgiveness and gratitude work together to counteract all of the destructive effects of anger and resentment.

The Health Effects of Anger vs. Forgiveness

This could be a book unto itself, so I will just give you the highlights. You can look online for the many scientific research studies that have been done on this.

Health Risks of Anger

Holding on to anger and resentment is really hard on the body and has been associated with:

- Migraines
- Digestion problems
- Insomnia
- Increased anxiety
- Depression
- High blood pressure
- Skin problems,
- Heart attack
- Stroke
- Poor immune response
- Diabetes
- Obesity
- Sexual dysfunction
- Brain fog / fatigue
- Suicidal thoughts

Not on this list, but well-known to everyone in a 12-step program is that resentment is one of the leading drivers of substance abuse, which can lead to all of the above and more. As the AA Big Book says: *"Resentment is the number one offender. It destroys more alcoholics than anything else."*

Alongside these physical problems, chronic anger and resentment also cause emotional problems:
- Low self-esteem
- Anxiety
- Relationship problems, including
- Emotional and physical abuse of others

All of these symptoms can then spill over into one's professional or work life, causing angry and resentful people to
- get passed by for promotions.
- not be chosen for team projects.
- intimidate or chase away clients and customers.
- make judgment errors when angry.

Health Benefits of Forgiveness and Gratitude

On the other hand, research has shown that forgiveness and an "attitude of gratitude" can physically

- lower the risk of heart attack.
- improve cholesterol levels.
- improve sleep.
- reduce the perception of pain.
- reduce blood pressure.
- reduce anxiety.
- reduce depression.

Emotionally, they can
- make you happier.
- improve your relationships.
- make people like you and enjoy being with you.
- improve romantic relationships.
- improve friendships.
- increase social support.
- improve family relationships.
- enhance other positive emotions.
- increase self-esteem.

- decrease suicidal thoughts.
- make you more optimistic.
- enhance your spirituality.
- make you more generous and compassionate.
- make you less materialistic.

Professionally, they can
- make us better managers and employees.
- reduce impatience and improve decision-making.
- renew our sense of purpose in our work.
- make us less likely to quit or be fired.
- reduce work stress.

Healing through Character Strengths

In the section on reframing our internal understanding of the experiences that made us angry, I listed a number of emotions that are often hiding behind our anger. These emotions represent the source of the original hurt that we then responded to with anger and resentment.

I said that each of these hidden emotions is a sign of a missing virtue or character strength that you need in order to heal. Naming them is the first step in finding their complement.

Negative emotions often feed our anger, so if we can develop the virtue or character strength that counteracts these emotions, then we will be less likely to become angry. We will also be much happier and healthier. We will also be more lovable people, which will make it easier to love ourselves, making it easier to forgive ourselves and others.

Fear is the absence of safety or security. We can combat it by "trusting in God and tying our camel." That is, we take precautions to protect ourselves physically and emotionally, then put our trust in God.

Anxiety is thought of as generalized fear without a focal point. My personal belief is that what we fear is that we have lost our way. We are adrift, and fear that if we don't discover our true purpose, something soul-crushing will happen to us that we can't quite name. The cure is to become confident in who we are and why we are here, and to have faith that, with God's help, we can achieve it.

Frustration is the absence of serenity – refusing to accept what actually *is* instead of what you want *right now*. Patience is required.

Confusion is a lack of clarity that can make us feel stupid. Slow down. Think it through. We can find the answer when we let go of the fear of getting it wrong.

Sadness means we have lost something of value. Honor what you have lost, then look for another source of that value. It won't be the same, but it will meet some of the same needs.

Isolation is a lack of connection and community. It takes effort. Commit to leaving the house for some social activity at least one night a week.

Guilt, well, we've talked about this. It requires forgiveness.

Shame – ditto.

Jealousy ends when we take joy in other people's good fortune.

Loneliness – to make a friend, be a friend – or forgive the ones you let go of.

Rejection hurts when we value other people's opinions of us more than our own. Know your worth.

Embarrassment reminds us that we are human and make mistakes. With confidence it is fleeting.

Humiliation is not possible when you know you are a noble, worthy human being. You cannot be defined by one mistake, no matter what it is.

Stress means you need serenity, faith, and self-care. Schedule time each day to take care of yourself and connect with God.

Helplessness comes from not claiming your powers and capacities and exerting your will.

Exhaustion just means you need rest. Self-care is a virtue. Sleep is a biological necessity. Mental exhaustion is just as real as the physical, so schedule mental relaxation as well as physical sleep.

Hunger means you need to remember to stop and eat.

I hope these brief descriptions don't sound flippant. Obviously, many books could be written about each of these emotions. The important point to hold on to is that positive emotions tell us that a virtue is present, and negative or painful emotions tell us that a virtue is missing. Every negative emotion and every negative experience can be healed by the application of one or more virtues or character strengths. Remember this when you are in pain, and it will point you towards a way to heal.

The Secret of Depression

The title of this book could almost as easily have been *The Secret of Depression*.

You may have noticed in the list above that one of the symptoms of chronic resentment is depression. There is a simple reason for that.

There is a school of thought that says that depression is actually *anger turned inward*. The first time I heard that, a light bulb went off in my head. You see, as I've said many times throughout this book, anger is the natural response to a perceived injustice.

When something bad happens to us, it sets off an internal battle between the part of us that wants to blame someone else and the part of us that thinks that we must have deserved whatever happened to us. If we allow ourselves to get angry, then the *"blame someone else"* side won. If we swallow the anger and turn it inward, then the *"it was my fault and I deserved it"* side won. In many cases, the battle never ends, and we blame both ourselves and others. If we don't process the anger in a healthy way, then we live forever feeling like all of the bad things that ever happened to us were our fault.

If they were our fault in the past, then they will be our fault going into the future. There is no hope. Nothing we do will improve our lives. We don't deserve happiness.

Sounds pretty depressing, doesn't it?

That's why I firmly believe that addressing anger and learning forgiveness are the two most effective tools for ending the epidemic of depression that is affecting virtually every country in the world.

Once our body is in a state of depression, anti-depressant drugs may be necessary to kick-start the brain's ability to feel pleasure. But that is just addressing the symptoms. The real cause of many people's depression is rampant injustice, repressed anger, and the inability to forgive.

How Can I Forgive Myself? Isn't That God's Right?

Talking with a friend about learning how to forgive ourselves, she asked, "What right do I have to forgive myself? Doesn't God decide who deserves forgiveness and who doesn't?"

If you believe in a vengeful God who punishes you when you make mistakes, then that might be one of the beliefs you will need to forgive someone for teaching you.

The God I believe in loves all of us and wants the best for everyone. God's "punishments" are actually given to us to help us understand when we've made a mistake. They are the natural consequences of doing something that is not an expression of our greatest good. (This is the subject of my book *Why Me? – A Spiritual Guide to Growing through Tests*.)

When we ask God for forgiveness, we are already acknowledging that we have made a mistake. We've grown and learned. Now we are asking God to minimize the natural consequences of our actions.

Maybe they will be minimized, maybe they won't. In either case, God is not piling on additional pain and suffering as a punishment. Whatever pain we feel is the result of our own actions.

When we forgive ourselves, we are not trying to escape the consequences of our actions – those have probably already been visited upon us. We are trying to escape the paralyzing sensation of shame that keeps us from moving forward. We know we made a mistake, or we wouldn't feel the shame, and we wouldn't be trying to forgive ourselves. We forgive ourselves when we accept that we are human and that we are allowed to make mistakes and learn from them. If God forgives us and wants the best for us, shouldn't we do the same?

Here is a short selection of prayers for forgiveness. Use them to forgive yourself. Use them to forgive others.

Prayers for Forgiveness

O Thou Provider, O Thou Forgiver! Grant us Thy grace and loving-kindness, Thy gifts and Thy bestowals, and sustain us, that we may attain our goal. Thou art the Powerful, the Able, the Knower, the Seer; and verily Thou art the Generous, and verily Thou art the All-Merciful, and verily Thou art the Ever-Forgiving, He to Whom repentance is due, He Who forgiveth even the most grievous of sins. –'Abdu'l-Bahá

Our Father, Who art in heaven, hallowed be Thy name; Thy kingdom come; Thy will be done; on earth as it is in heaven. Give us this day our daily bread, and forgive us our trespasses, as we forgive those who trespass against us. And lead us not into temptation; but deliver us from evil. For Thine is the kingdom, the power and the glory, for ever and ever. Amen. –Christian Prayer

My Lord, forgive me and accept my repentance, You are the Ever-Relenting, the All-Forgiving. –Islamic Prayer

Our God and God of our ancestors! Let our prayers come before You and do not hide Yourself from our supplication. For neither are we so arrogant nor hardened to say, "We are righteous and have not sinned," for truly, truly, we have sinned. May it be Your will, O Lord our God, to forgive all our sins, and pardon all our iniquities. –Jewish Prayer

I beg Thee to forgive me, O my Lord, for every mention but the mention of Thee, and for every praise but the praise of Thee, and for every delight but delight in Thy nearness, and for every pleasure but the pleasure of communion with Thee, and for every joy but the joy of Thy love and of Thy good-pleasure, and for all things pertaining unto me which bear no relationship unto Thee, O Thou Who art the Lord of lords, He Who provideth the means and unlocketh the doors. –The Báb

O Thou forgiving Lord! Thou art the shelter of all these Thy servants. Thou knowest the secrets and art aware of all things. We are all helpless, and Thou art the Mighty, the Omnipotent. We are all sinners, and Thou art the Forgiver of sins, the Merciful, the Compassionate. O Lord! Look not at our shortcomings. Deal with us according to Thy grace and bounty. Our shortcomings are many, but the ocean of Thy forgiveness is boundless. Our weakness is grievous, but the evidences of Thine aid and assistance are clear. Therefore, confirm and strengthen us. Enable us to do that which is worthy of Thy holy Threshold. Illumine our hearts, grant us discerning eyes and attentive ears. Resuscitate the dead and heal the sick. Bestow wealth upon the poor and give peace and security to the fearful. Accept us in Thy kingdom and illumine us with the light of guidance. Thou art the Powerful and the Omnipotent. Thou art the Generous. Thou art the Clement. Thou art the Kind. –'Abdu'l Bahá

Prayer for Parents

I beg Thy forgiveness, O my God, and implore pardon after the manner Thou wishest Thy servants to direct themselves to Thee. I beg of Thee to wash away our sins as befitteth Thy Lordship, and to forgive me, my parents, and those who in Thy estimation have entered the abode of Thy love in a manner which is worthy of Thy transcendent sovereignty and well beseemeth the glory of Thy celestial power.

O my God! Thou hast inspired my soul to offer its supplication to Thee, and but for Thee, I would not call upon Thee. Lauded and glorified art Thou; I yield Thee praise inasmuch as Thou didst reveal Thyself unto me, and I beg Thee to forgive me, since I have fallen short in my duty to know Thee and have failed to walk in the path of Thy love. –The Báb

Prayers for Serenity

> O God! Refresh and gladden my spirit. Purify my heart. Illumine my powers. I lay all my affairs in Thy hand. Thou art my Guide and my Refuge. I will no longer be sorrowful and grieved; I will be a happy and joyful being. O God! I will no longer be full of anxiety, nor will I let trouble harass me. I will not dwell on the unpleasant things of life. O God! Thou art more friend to me than I am to myself. I dedicate myself to Thee, O Lord. —Bahá'í Prayer

> God, grant me the serenity to accept the things I cannot change, courage to change the things I can, and wisdom to know the difference. —Reinhold Niebuhr

Prayer for Healing

> Thy name is my healing, O my God, and remembrance of Thee is my remedy. Nearness to Thee is my hope, and love for Thee is my companion. Thy mercy to me is my healing and my succor in both this world and the world to come. Thou, verily, art the All-Bountiful, the All-Knowing, the All-Wise.
> —Bahá'u'lláh

An Assortment of Quotations about Forgiveness

What Is Forgiveness?

"Forgiving is...recognizing the injury, owning the pain, & reaching out." —David W Augsburger

"How does one know if she has forgiven? You tend to feel sorrow over the circumstance instead of rage, you tend to feel sorry for the person rather than angry with him. You tend to have nothing left to say about it all." —Clarissa Pinkola Estés

"Forgiveness is an act of the will, and the will can function regardless of the temperature of the heart." —Corrie Ten Boom

"Inner peace can be reached only when we practice forgiveness. Forgiveness is letting go of the past, and is therefore the means for correcting our misperceptions."
—Gerald G. Jampolsky

Forgiveness Sets You Free

"I think the first step is to understand that forgiveness does not exonerate the perpetrator. Forgiveness liberates the victim. It's a gift you give yourself." –T. D. Jakes

"When you hold resentment toward another, you are bound to that person or condition by an emotional link that is stronger than steel. Forgiveness is the only way to dissolve that link and get free." –Catherine Ponder

"To forgive is the highest, most beautiful form of love. In return, you will receive untold peace and happiness."
–Robert Muller

"As I walked out the door toward the gate that would lead to my freedom, I knew if I didn't leave my bitterness and hatred behind, I'd still be in prison." –Nelson Mandela

"Resentment is like drinking poison and then hoping it will kill your enemies." –Nelson Mandela

"To forgive is to set a prisoner free and discover that the prisoner was you." –Louis B. Smedes

"Let go. Why do you cling to pain? There is nothing you can do about the wrongs of yesterday. It is not yours to judge. Why hold on to the very thing which keeps you from hope and love?" –Leo Buscaglia

"Forgive others not because they deserve forgiveness, but because you deserve peace." –Jonathan Huie

"Forgiveness is the key that unlocks the door of resentment and the handcuffs of hatred. It is a power that breaks the chains of bitterness and the shackles of selfishness."
–Corrie Ten Boom

"There is a hard law. When an injury is done to us, we never recover until we forgive. " –Alan Paton

"I eventually came to understand that in harboring the anger, the bitterness and resentment towards those that had hurt me, I was giving the reins of control over to them. Forgiving was not about accepting their words and deeds. Forgiving was about letting go and moving on with my life. In doing so, I had finally set myself free." –Isabel Lopez

Love Yourself First

"How unhappy is he who cannot forgive himself."
–Publilius Syrus

"The remarkable thing is that we really love our neighbour as ourselves: we do unto others as we do unto ourselves. We hate others when we hate ourselves. We are tolerant toward others when we tolerate ourselves. We forgive others when we forgive ourselves. We are prone to sacrifice others when we are ready to sacrifice ourselves." –Eric Hoffer

"I think that if God forgives us we must forgive ourselves. Otherwise, it is almost like setting up ourselves as a higher tribunal than Him." –C.S. Lewis

"Love is forgiving, accepting, moving on, embracing, and all encompassing. And if you're not doing that for yourself, you cannot do that with anyone else." –Steve Maraboli,

"Letting ourselves be forgiven is one of the most difficult healings we will undertake. And one of the most fruitful."
–Stephen Levine

Being Heard Is the Key

"The first duty of love is to listen." –Paul Tillich

"Too often we underestimate the power of a touch, a smile, a kind word, a listening ear, an honest compliment, or the smallest act of caring, all of which have the potential to turn a life around." –Leo Buscaglia

"Listening is a gift of spiritual significance that you can learn to give to others. When you listen, you give one a sense of importance, hope and love that he or she may not receive any other way. Through listening, we nurture and validate the feelings one has, especially when he or she experiences difficulties in life." –H. Norman Wright

"Listening to one another activates our mirror neurons and resonance circuitry, so that we can be said to literally begin to inhabit one another's embodied emotional universe."
–Bonnie Badenoch

"Sometimes all a person wants is an empathetic ear; all he or she needs is to talk it out. Just offering a listening ear and an understanding heart for his or her suffering can be a big comfort." — Roy T. Bennett

"An open ear is the only believable sign of an open heart."
–David W Augsburger

"Your inner child needs non-shaming ally to validate his abandonment, neglect, abuse, and enmeshment. Those are the first essential elements in original pain work." –John Bradshaw

Forgiveness Makes Us Better People

"The weak can never forgive. Forgiveness is the attribute of the strong." –Mahatma Gandhi

"Anger makes you smaller, while forgiveness forces you to grow beyond what you were." –Cherie Carter-Scott

"Be the one who nurtures and builds. Be the one who has an understanding and a forgiving heart one who looks for the best in people. Leave people better than you found them."
–Marvin J. Ashton

"Forgiveness does not change the past, but it does enlarge the future." –Paul Boose

"We must be willing to let go of the life we've planned, so as to have the life that is waiting for us." –Joseph Campbell

"You can clutch the past so tightly to your chest that it leaves your arms too full to embrace the present."
–Jan Glidewell

"Grudges are for those who insist that they are owed something; forgiveness, however, is for those who are substantial enough to move on." –Criss Jami, Salomé

"If I could forgive, it meant I was a strong good person who could take responsibility for the path I had chosen for myself, and all the consequences that accompanied that choice. And it gave me the simple but powerful satisfaction of extending a kindness to another person in a tough spot."
–Piper Kerman

"Love people who hate you. Pray for people who have wronged you. It won't just change their life...it'll change yours."
–Mandy Hale

"The willingness to forgive is a sign of spiritual and emotional maturity. It is one of the great virtues to which we all should aspire. Imagine a world filled with individuals willing both to apologize and to accept an apology. Is there any problem that could not be solved among people who possessed the humility and largeness of spirit and soul to do either — or both — when needed?" –Gordon B. Hinckley

"When we think we have been hurt by someone in the past, we build up defenses to protect ourselves from being hurt in the future. So the fearful past causes a fearful future and the past and future become one. We cannot love when we feel fear.... When we release the fearful past and forgive everyone, we will experience total love and oneness with all."
–Gerald G. Jampolsky

Forgiveness Heals Relationships

"Forgiveness is a sign that the person who has wronged you means more to you than the wrong they have dealt."
–Ben Greenhalgh

"A broken friendship that is mended through forgiveness can be even stronger than it once was." –Stephen Richards

"A heart filled with anger has no room for love."
–Joan Lunden

"There isn't time, so brief is life, for bickerings, apologies, heartburnings, callings to account. There is only time for loving, and but an instant, so to speak, for that." –Mark Twain

"For there are two kinds of forgiveness in the world: the one you practice because everything really is all right, and what went before is mended. The other kind of forgiveness you practice because someone needs desperately to be forgiven, or because you need just as badly to forgive them, for a heart can grab hold of old wounds and go sour as milk over them."
–Catherynne M. Valente

"Apologizing does not always mean you're wrong and the other person is right. It just means you value your relationship more than your ego." –Mark Matthews

"It's all very well to tell us to forgive our enemies; our enemies can never hurt us very much. But oh, what about forgiving our friends?" –Willa Cather

Forgiveness Requires Empathy

Before we can forgive one another, we have to understand one another. –Emma Goldman

To understand somebody else as a human being, I think, is about as close to real forgiveness as one can get. –David Small

"You don't need strength to let go of something. What you really need is understanding." –Guy Finley

"I can always forgive where I understand." –Jude Morgan

"You will know that forgiveness has begun when you recall those who hurt you and feel the power to wish them well."
–Lewis B. Smedes

"You can't forgive without loving. And I don't mean sentimentality. I don't mean mush. I mean having enough courage to stand up and say, 'I forgive. I'm finished with it.'"
–Maya Angelou

"When you begin to see that your enemy is suffering, that is the beginning of insight." –Thich Nhat Hanh

"We are all mistaken sometimes; sometimes we do wrong things, things that have bad consequences. But it does not mean we are evil, or that we cannot be trusted ever afterward."
–Alison Croggon

"Each person you meet is an aspect of yourself, clamoring for love." –Eric Micha'el Leventhal

Anger Is Valid

"When we forgive evil we do not excuse it, we do not tolerate it, we do not smother it. We look the evil full in the face, call it what it is, let its horror shock and stun and enrage us, and only then do we forgive it." –Lewis B. Smedes

"Anger is like flowing water; there's nothing wrong with it as long as you let it flow. Hate is like stagnant water; anger that you denied yourself the freedom to feel, the freedom to flow; water that you gathered in one place and left to forget. Stagnant water becomes dirty, stinky, disease-ridden, poisonous, deadly; that is your hate. On flowing water travels little paper boats; paper boats of forgiveness. Allow yourself to feel anger, allow your waters to flow, along with all the paper boats of forgiveness. Be human." –C. JoyBell C.

"Anger is an essential part of being human. People are taught to deny themselves anger, and in this, they are actually opening themselves up to hate. The more you deny yourself the freedom to be angry, the more you will hate. Let yourself be angry, and hate will disintegrate, and when hate disintegrates, forgiveness prevails! The more you deny that you are angry, in attempts to be "holy" the more inhuman you will become, and the more inhuman you will become, the harder it will be to forgive." –C. JoyBell C.

Miscellaneous Insights

"[D]on't cling to your self-righteous suffering, let it go…. Nothing is too good to be true, let yourself be forgiven. To the degree you insist that you must suffer, you insist on the suffering of others as well." —Stephen Levine

"People have a core need to know they are significant to others and it is central to how people see themselves at an identity level. I maintain that you really can't be satisfied in life without the feeling of matter to others." –Gordon Flett

"Every child needs desperately to know that s/he matters to his parents. Mattering means that the child's specialness is reflected in the eyes of his parents or other significant caretakers. Mattering is also indicated by the amount of time they spend with him. Children know intuitively that people give time to what they love." –John Bradshaw

"The frustration of a child's desire to be loved as a person and to have his love accepted is the greatest trauma that a child can experience." –John Bradshaw

"The spiritual wound can be healed. But it must be done by grieving, and that is painful." –John Bradshaw

"One of the reasons we have sadness is to complete painful events of the past, so that our energy can be available for the present. When we are not allowed to grieve, the energy is frozen." –John Bradshaw

"Simply touching a difficult memory with some slight willingness to heal begins to soften the holding and tension around it." —Stephen Levine

"There is a saying that to understand is to forgive, but that is an error, so Papa used to say. You must forgive in order to understand. Until you forgive, you defend yourself against the possibility of understanding. ...If you forgive, he would say, you may indeed still not understand, but you will be ready to understand, and that is the posture of grace."
–Marilynne Robinson

"Forgiveness is the economy of the heart....forgiveness saves the expense of anger, the cost of hatred, the waste of spirits." –Hannah More

"If you understood how frequently people cope by projecting, you would learn to take absolutely nothing personally."
–Jesica Nodarse

Without forgiveness life is governed by an endless cycle of resentment and retaliation. –Roberto Assagioli

"Forgiveness is the only way to reverse the irreversible flow of history." –Hannah Arendt

"The practice of forgiveness is our most important contribution to the healing of the world." –Marianne Williamson